One day Tim, a very dear friend of ours, arrived with the dreadful news that his best friend had committed suicide. He was full of questions about God and heaven, looking for answers to why something like this had happened.

Though I desperately wanted to help Tim, I didn't have the answers. I believed in God and went to church, but no words of comfort came to me. I was numb. The only thing I could do was listen, but that wasn't enough and I knew it.

When Tim left I felt a cold, dark emptiness settle over me. Wasn't there an answer anywhere for those of us who weren't coping?

Take Me Home

BONNIE JAMISON

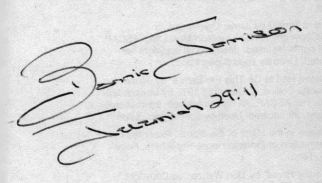

LIVING BOOKS
Tyndale House Publishers, Inc.
Wheaton, Illinois

Second printing, April 1986
Library of Congress Catalog Card Number 85-51840
ISBN 0-8423-6901-5
Copyright 1985 by Bonnie Jamison
All rights reserved
Printed in the United States of America

It is only natural for me to dedicate this book with my love to Ted and our three children, John, Lisa, and Brooke. They unselfishly contributed enormously by lightening the weight of the responsibility of caring for my mother. I thank God every day that he gave them to me to love and cherish.

Take Me Home has been affectionately dedicated to many people. Prominent among them is Toni, who saw my need and knew there was only One who could fill it. To this day she is a shining example of a quiet, gentle instrument of God continuing to show others that there is a better way. She remains my precious friend and I love her.

To God—may he receive the glory for all he has done.

Contents

Acknowledgments

The following people have significantly contributed to this book. They are acknowledged here with gratitude and love.

To my husband, Ted, and our children, John, Lisa, and Brooke who excused my absences, forgave the late dinners, and listened attentively, patiently, and with humor when I shared my work.

To Toni Williams, who taught me what it meant to depend on God as I watched him stretch me wider and higher than ever before. She laughed with me, cried with me, and spent endless hours correcting my English while offering practical suggestions

To Rita Baker, whose valuable professional knowledge gave the book the polish it needed. From her I gained much. Most of all, a wonderful gift from God.

To Don, Toni's husband, who gave untold hours to help me understand the word processor that he unselfishly loaned to me. Without it, I might have given up. And Eric and Trevor, Toni and Don's sons, who welcomed this writer into their lives at the strangest hours of the day, answered questions when Don wasn't around, and separated numerous copies to save me time.

To Doug Suriano, my son-in-law, who gave me hugs of encouragement and assured me that he was praying.

To everyone whose name is written on the pages of this book. Without them there wouldn't be a story.

To Bob Rhodes, my first creative writing teacher, whose encouraging words, "Anyone who has a story can write," made the difference.

To Joan Jaggard, Pat Gareau, Dan Galvin, and Nancy Schumacher who spent time reading my manuscript and offered their valuable opinions.

To those who took seriously my "prayer letter," to the "Joy in the Morning" Bible study, our "dinner friends," and the Pinelands Christian Women's Club who prayed for me faithfully for the fifteen months I worked on this book. Everyone prayed not only that God's will would be accomplished, but that my physical, emotional, and spiritual needs would be met; and they were.

To Mrs. Umpehent, a dear, precious lady who lived in a nursing home and told me she wanted to pray for me. I know she did and that her prayers were answered.

To Marlene Bagnull, whose ethical professionalism enriched me. Her example as an accomplished Christian writer continues to inspire and motivate me.

To Virginia Muir, whom God placed in my life at just the right time. She gave me the extra push that I needed and then corrected my work with wisdom. And to Karen Ball, my editor at Tyndale House, who tightened and strengthened my work.

My thanks to all of you!

Introduction

This book has been written from my heart to yours. It is very personal, permitting you a private look into the lives of our family during a time of decision when the wrong choice could have brought crises.

The printed pages are shared to encourage those of you who have had your lives suddenly interrupted by an unexpected invasion of the terminal illness of a loved one.

I do not want to minimize the complexities of caring for a terminal patient. Rather, my prayer is that you will recognize that your own keen, discerning wisdom is insufficient to meet the challenging road that lies before you. May you turn to God for guidance. If you do, you will see that the strength, the durability, and the rewarding pathway he gave to me can be yours for the asking. Only then will you discover that when your years together slip rapidly into moments, you can learn valuable lessons.

I am convinced that the underlying problem of loneliness and estrangement that terminal patients and their loved ones feel can be dealt with completely when they come face to face with the living Lord Jesus Christ. When this occurs, their goals are changed and deep relationships with God and each other are nurtured. Strengthened by the experience, they will turn toward a new horizon and discover a fresh, new purpose for living.

Suffering should never be wasted by bowing to the "why me's," the "if only's," and the "pity parties" of life. Suffering has the potential of showing us how to go through the valleys of life where death's shadows cast a light of truth that will encourage others filled with despair. Though suffering and loss may occur, victory can be won under God's watchful love and care.

Certain names in the following pages have been changed to protect privacy.

Therefore whosoever heareth these sayings of mine, and doeth them, I will liken him unto a wise man, which built his house upon a rock: And the rain descended, and the floods came, and the winds blew, and beat upon that house; and it fell not; for it was founded upon a rock (Matthew 7:24, 25).

1
A Dreadful Silence

I was dumb with silence, I held my peace, even from good; and my sorrow was stirred (Psalm 39:2).

I found myself hypnotically staring out the kitchen window as the ringing phone interrupted my drifting, idle thoughts.

Wiping my wet hands on a damp tea towel, I picked up the receiver.

"Hello."

"Bonnie," my sister said, "I think it would be a good idea if you came down to see Mother. She seems to be failing rapidly, and a visit from you might lift her spirits a little. Also, I have serious doubts about the nursing home and some financial questions need answers quickly. Only you and I can make the necessary decisions."

After a few more minutes of conversation, we hung up and I sat wondering how I'd ever work out the details of another trip south.

How many times I'd driven down to visit Mother "for the last time." Whenever Sandy called, there was always a sense of urgency in her voice. I had just been there several weeks ago, and now again!

I didn't want to go back . . . back to facing a dying mother and the mounting difficulties that each new day seemed to produce. I deeply resented the demands that Mother's illness placed on all of us, and I hated myself for thinking such thoughts. Even more, I resented Mother's unrealistic, uncooperative approach to the problems she was facing. I always had the impression that everything we did wasn't suitable to Mother, thus causing dissatisfaction on both sides. I was withering from the traveling and all the decisions. With each visit I agonized more and more over the intensified complications that her illness created in our personal lives.

It was never easy getting away, even for a few days. I felt my place was at home keeping things going smoothly. I liked everything neat and in its proper place, and it was a full-time job keeping it that way. I was happiest when our lives were structured by schedules. Privacy was extremely important to me. All of this driving back and forth was causing confusion and disorder, and I found it exhausting.

Our oldest child, John, was fifteen and had just taken his very first summer job packing corn at a local farm. He needed me to drive him to and from work each day. I had to consider my husband also. After all, he needed me, if for nothing more than to be there when he came home at night. I knew he would manage; he always had before. Still, how much longer could this go on? No matter how many times I turned the situation over in my mind, I always wanted to stay home and care for my family. Wasn't that my primary responsibility?

The following morning I was all packed and ready to go when I glanced out the kitchen window and noticed John walking slowly across the yard toward the back door. It was only ten in the morning. His face was flushed and it appeared as though he had been crying. He looked disheveled and obviously upset.

He slammed the door behind him and slumped over the kitchen table, his reddened face drooping toward the floor.

"What's wrong?" I asked. He stubbornly refused to comment. "Why are you home so early?" I prodded. "Did something happen?"

"I quit!" he blurted. "I hate that darn job. The man is like a taskmaster and he says I can't do anything right. Today we were assembling the corn crates and he told me I wasn't making them fast enough. I've never constructed a corn crate in my life. How am I supposed to be able to do it without some instruction?" Disappointment and frustration were written all over his face. His first job, and after two days he felt like a failure.

Here I was getting ready to go away and he needed me more than ever. How could I leave him at a time like this? What in the world was I supposed to do now? I didn't know whether to leave him or take him along, but I had to come up with a solution in a hurry.

Interrupting my husband, Ted, at the office was something I never liked to do, but this time I had no choice. When I called and told him about my dilemma, his reaction was controlled and helpful.

"Go on down, Bonnie. Tell John to stay there until I get home and I'll take care of the situation then. Don't let this problem interfere with your plans."

John retreated to his room and I left with my daughters, Lisa and Brooke. I felt extremely uneasy about leaving, but was reassured that Ted would do just as he said he would.

Torn, always torn!

It was July 1976. For two years Mother had been transported periodically from my sister Sandy's house to mine and back again. Because Mother's care was becoming increasingly involved, Sandy and I shared the responsibility. As much as we tried not to let it show, caring for Mother for long periods of time caused overwhelming strains in our families.

In the beginning, the failure in Mother's

physical condition was subtle. So subtle that I was unaware of any problem until the summer of 1972 when Sandy came home for a visit and asked me, "What's wrong with Mother, Bonnie?"

"What do you mean?" I asked.

"Can't you hear the slurring in her speech?"

"No," I said. "I'll have to listen to her more carefully." I wasn't instantly alarmed, just concerned.

We both knew that broaching a subject like this to Mother was like walking on thin ice. We had to treat the matter very delicately. We knew she would deny any problem because of her beliefs as a Christian Scientist.

Through the Christian Science teachings, Mother had come to believe that all sickness and suffering were illusions which could be overcome by "right thinking," by seeking union with God. To Mother, evil and the material world had no real existence; God was spirit, therefore man also was spirit since he was made in God's image. The physical body and all its physical problems were just figments of man's imagination.

However, shortly after Sandy's observation, I approached Mother with the sensitive subject.

"Mother," I said with reservation, "Sandy told me that she detected a little problem with your speech. She thought possibly you might be slurring your words a bit." Mother sat quietly listening. "Are you having any difficulty that you'd like to talk about? Do you have any pain or discomfort?"

"No," she said quickly, while observing me curiously and answering exactly the way I'd expected.

"How do you really feel, Mother?"

"I feel just fine," she said, again with the curious look. Mother was never one to question my motives.

I knew better than to try to carry the subject much further. She wouldn't allow the conversation to go below the surface.

"Mother, would you object if I took a quick look inside your mouth? Maybe there's something I could see that you can't feel."

Confident that nothing was wrong, she allowed me to look inside her mouth. Her willingness to permit this surprised me. Checking carefully, I observed nothing out of the ordinary. Laughing, I admitted that I felt totally inadequate when it came to oral examinations and suggested the dentist.

With no hesitation, Mother made the appointment and went the following week. The dentist found nothing wrong. But the problem persisted and grew worse as the years slipped by.

Sandy and I both were sure that Mother's difficulty had begun six months before we noticed the slurring, when Mother, then age fifty-seven, had been involved in a serious auto accident. She must have lost her concentration, because she hit a car head on, never braking. She struck her head against the windshield and crushed the steering wheel with her body. Her car was totally destroyed.

Mother refused to go to a hospital. Instead, she was taken to her apartment by a close friend who just happened to be passing the scene at the time of the accident.

When I arrived at Mother's apartment a short while later, I found her lying motionless in her bed. She smiled warmly and I knew she was happy to see me. However, she had a very peculiar look in her eyes. They were eyes that held hurt, maybe even pain. There were several cuts on her face and she told me her back was bothering her. Nevertheless, she was physically better than I'd expected . . . but, those eyes. It was as though they wanted to say what her mouth refused to admit.

Were there internal injuries? I doubted I'd ever know. Yet, for the sake of my own conscience, I had to ask her if she would allow me to take her to a doctor for a quick check-up.

Mother's deeply rooted beliefs kept her from making the decision to go, and I found myself yielding again to her doctrine. The entire time I was with her that day, she never complained of pain. All she asked was that I call her practitioner, a person schooled in the beliefs of Christian Science. She supported Mother during difficult times by praying, reading, encouraging, and fortifying the doctrines of their common faith.

Slowly Mother's body seemed to heal with little visible discomfort. She exhibited no signs of any serious aftermath. Only a small scar remained on her chin. Her back, which had always given her problems, didn't seem any worse from the accident. She was considered very fortunate!

Tears blurred my vision as I strained to focus on my speedometer while traveling down the turnpike the day after Sandy's insistent phone call. I was pleased that my daughters sat so quietly amusing themselves because I wasn't in the mood for rowdiness. Even light conversation would have intruded on my thoughts.

Today I couldn't control the deeply discouraging and disheartening feelings that echoed through my mind. I couldn't shake the chilling thought that Mother was dying. Would this be my last trip south?

For me, the most dreaded aspect of living was dying. I was terrified of the word *death*. I thought it was a hideous word—so permanent, final, and forever. I found it easier to tuck that word into the far corners of my mind, but it kept subtly creeping back, haunting me. It loomed ahead of me now, casting foreboding shadows over my entire trip.

When we finally arrived at my sister's, I was beginning to feel better. Since Sandy had made an appointment with the administrator of the nursing home to discuss the finances, we decided to head directly there.

As we drove into the parking lot, I didn't find anything too different or unusual about this nursing home. I was neither favorably nor unfavorably impressed. It was adequate. Once I passed through the doors, though, I detected an air of suppressed insensitivity, and my stomach felt queasy. Something was wrong. Maybe I was uncomfortable knowing my own mother had to be here. I was unable to put my finger on the problem.

We walked down the wide, drab hallway, the children beside us. The painful screams of suffering human beings made the reality of death too close for comfort.

As we drew closer to Mother's room, Sandy pointed to her doorway and we walked through. I let my eyes move hesitantly toward Mother, half afraid of what I'd see. A lump formed in my throat as I slowly registered the changes. Her wide grin steadied my focus and I struggled to return the smile. All the while my heart sobbed; I felt like it was breaking apart.

"Hi, Mother," I said softly. I noticed a blush

of color come into her face, and then a glowing hope made tears swell in her eyes.

Those same eyes caught the children, and delight spread even further across her face as they ran to her bed. It was a typical happy reunion. Being a family who always expressed itself with much emotion and affection, we smothered her with hugs and kisses. Touching Mother was important and necessary; it made her feel better about herself and showed her that we weren't repulsed by her sickness. Her blue eyes sparkled despite her condition.

Seeing Mother again caused me to reflect for a moment on how much had happened since Sandy had first noticed Mother's speech affliction several years ago. As it became even more pronounced, we also began to see evidence of increasing physical debility. She experienced weakness, became tired very easily, and lost her balance frequently. She fell sound asleep on a couch right in the middle of a jubilant family reunion. She tripped on numerous occasions, and one time, while at Sandy's, she fell down a full flight of stairs. She walked with tremendous difficulty. She had long since given up driving. Her body was failing her, yet our hands continued to be tied because of her refusal to seek an accurate and complete diagnosis.

For the time being we convinced ourselves that a nursing home was the answer. It afforded us time to think about the direction in which we were headed.

When we listened very carefully as Mother spoke, Sandy and I could still understand most of what she said. However, everyone else understood Mother only when she took the painstaking patience to write her message on paper. She had grown immeasurably limited.

I knew there had to be times when she felt concern, as well as alarm, as the slow process of muscular deterioration advanced. My thoughts had been confirmed when, a few years earlier, Mother revealed that she had made an appointment to see a doctor.

"Just a diagnosis, mind you," Mother explained. "There will be no treatment. Christian Science permits a diagnosis. Nevertheless, I want it to remain a secret." I was perplexed, yet relieved, when she told me of her decision.

She had chosen a doctor who was also her cousin, knowing she had his deepest respect and confidence and that he wouldn't breathe a word to anyone. Her fear of others knowing was tremendous. In her mind, seeing a doctor was a sign of weakness and defeat.

"No one is to know!" she reiterated.

After the appointment, I called the doctor personally.

"Bonnie, I've examined your mother thoroughly and suspect Landry's Ascending Paralysis or Guillain-Barre Syndrome. Your mother exhibits all the characteristics of this rapidly progressive and acute form of polyneuropathy. I observed muscular weakness and mild distal sensory loss."

Nothing he said made sense to me. Nevertheless, I felt fear grip me.

"Just what does all of this mean?" I asked.

"This disease, Landry's Paralysis, is considered a medical emergency and requires constant attention. Bonnie, your mother will never survive without medical treatment. Even with it, her chances are slim. From my observation, she's in an advanced stage and her life expectancy is perhaps six months. This disease kills quickly."

I was stunned! My mother dead in six months? How could that possibly be?

"What do you suggest we do?" I asked, trying to get a grasp on all he'd said.

"While your mother was here today, I made an appointment with the chief of neurology at the hospital where I practice. He is an extremely competent man and can quickly determine her condition. We must be certain. I explained the urgency, and he's coming into his office on Saturday, just to see her. Let's pray that she doesn't change her mind."

The following morning Mother called the doctor and canceled her appointment. There was no convincing her otherwise. She stood firm. She was determined to do it her way!

Mother had always treasured a fierce independence, proud of the fact that she'd successfully earned her own way through most of her life.

As a young woman, Mother had been radiantly beautiful . . . gorgeous by many people's standards. She had blonde wavy hair and very delicate blue eyes that sparkled when she laughed and deepened in color when she grew serious. Her complexion was like that of a china doll, smooth and white. She always dressed in meticulous fashion, spoke eloquently, and had an animated, effervescent personality. She was bright and intelligent, possessed a rare quality of gentleness, and a genuine concern for others. She was committed to reaching out to anyone in need. Consumed with constant activity, she was happiest when she was aggressively involved in the lives of others.

When I was a baby, she and my dad had divorced. For years she played the dual role of mother and father. During those years she'd acquired an excellent reputation as a registered nurse. She was highly respected for her professionalism, and spent years nursing many elderly, influential people, caring for them until their deaths.

Mother always kept us informed about her personal and occupational life, openly sharing her joys and sorrows. Our home was richly blessed and I felt very secure in her love.

"Mommy," our maternal grandmother, shared our warm, comfortable home with us. We were fortunate to have had her because she provided just the right atmosphere during the long hours Mother spent working. Mommy had been the experienced mother of eight children herself and she was acutely aware of what it would take to help us through the challenging years that were ahead. She was like a precious gift from God, infusing gems of wisdom into our lives. Many times I felt closer to her than I did to my own mother.

When I was twelve years old, Mother remarried. From that point on our lives took on new, exciting, yet sometimes drastic, changes. Our stepfather was winsome and kind. He became a sound, dependable member of our family.

A year after their marriage, a son was born, delighting us all as only a baby can. Our home became more complete and the marriage proved to be solid, lasting only seven short years before "Daddy" became ill and died.

Then came the greatest changes of all within my mother. After so many years of providing medical care as a nurse, Mother was introduced to Christian Science. Immediately, she became fanatical toward its teachings and claimed an "instantaneous healing" on her arthritic back. She avidly embraced Christian Science doctrine and radically altered her views about illness and medical treatment. There was no compromise. Eventually, she became a reader in her church as well as a practitioner.

Through all of this, Mother had developed a strong and independent character. Now, however, her inability to care for herself made her dependent on the kindness of the nurses in the nursing home. Would they have the time that was required to listen to her needs? Were they really enough?

As I drew up a chair, I put my head close to Mother's face.

"How are they treating you, Mother?" I asked quietly.

She nodded with half-hearted approval and gave the appearance of helplessness. I could sense a painful adjustment was taking place just by the look in her eyes. She so desperately wanted to talk as she lay there, covered with coarse sheets, surrounded by chalky pictureless walls, cold linoleum floors, and undraped windows. It was all so different from the elegance to which she had been accustomed.

I rambled on, talking just to keep the room from being too quiet. I hated silence! I tried to cheer Mother and build up her confidence, yet there hung around her a heavy weight of solemn suffering.

Time definitely was running out. How could we combat the ravages of this illness? Her life seemed suddenly compressed into a minute time capsule. At that moment, I determined that if we were the caring family we said we were, she would never suffer this disease alone. We would be there to help, somehow, some way!

In a place like this, it must be so easy to feel forsaken and lost. I could keenly sense Mother's desperation for the assurance that we cared about what was happening. Yet she continued to have such strong willpower, desire, belief . . . whatever it was, it was pulling her through.

My thoughts were interrupted when the children returned to the room eager to share what they had discovered during their investigation of the premises. Their attention, however, was drawn to their "Nanna," chatting with her as if she was able to respond. They were undaunted by her inability to talk distinctly or to be understood easily. They readily took the expressions from her face in place of any verbal response. Carefully, she listened with her eyes as well as her ears, absorbing their every word.

Our younger daughter, ten-year-old Brooke, was particularly adept at sharing enthusiastically with her grandmother. It brought me great joy to listen to her happy conversation and to see their easy communication. Cheerful tones were directed to "Nanna," who was the children's captive audience.

"It's time for our appointment with the administrator," Sandy finally said, and the two of us walked toward the door. I turned back and watched as the children continued their discussion, huddled around Mother's bedside, so absorbed that they were unaware we were leaving. Such innocence and tenderness created a picture of love that will remain securely etched in my mind.

After Sandy and I straightened out all the financial details, I decided to visit the head nurse. I was anxious to get her opinion of how Mother was adjusting to her new environment.

I entered the nurses' quarters and asked for the head nurse. She was busy doing some paperwork as I approached her desk. She stood up, and with a forced, somewhat mechanical smile introduced herself and asked if she could be of assistance.

When I explained why I had come, she assured me that Mother was adapting beautifully and I shouldn't be concerned about anything.

"Everyone on duty is highly trained, fully qualified, and thoroughly skilled to care for every situation," she said confidently and somewhat tersely.

Out of the corner of my eye I noticed another nurse nearby. The setting made me strangely ill at ease.

Becoming even more uncomfortable, I thanked her for her time, turned quickly, and walked out the door.

I felt placed in an awkward position. Mother was in a very vulnerable situation and I didn't like it. Somehow, I knew I could never grow accustomed to the highly impersonal style of this nursing home. I found it dehumanizing. I tried to picture how I'd feel if this were me here and not Mother. *Abandoned*, I thought. There was no other word for it.

The more I thought about it, the more difficult the situation became. My heart was pounding and my mind was racing to devise a way to remove Mother from this place.

Stepping briskly toward Mother's room, I could still hear those painful cries and moans coming from the rooms further down the hall. Picturing the despair of these people made the sounds seem even worse, and my determination grew stronger.

Suddenly I heard steps moving up behind me and a quiet voice whispered, "Miss?"

I turned around and there stood the nurse who had been nearby while I was having the discussion with the head nurse.

She looked at me with a gentle smile and in a hushed tone said, "Don't worry about your mom. I'll watch over her every day. Some of the nurses around here are very peculiar people!"

Then she moved quickly past me and slipped into the next room.

Her words swept over me like a cool refreshing breeze. I felt encouraged and I smiled, grateful for what she'd said and calmed by her compassion. At least there was someone in this place who understood. Even so, my uneasiness remained strong.

We still had no certainty as to the nature of Mother's progressive illness. I felt not only fear of the unknown disease, but anger and resentment toward Mother because she refused to recognize it as reality. After four years, she was still exhibiting denial and isolation.

Disillusionment and faltering expectations about the prospect of Mother's future in this nursing home again wrapped me so tightly I couldn't even think clearly. My impulse was to take Mother home, but the fear of a lingering illness kept me still. I forced myself to put a smile on my face, pretending that everything was going to be all right. I felt a protective love for Mother as I walked through the doorway into her room.

Sandy and I would have to deal honestly with Mother's situation. Without discussing my feelings, I tentatively suggested to Mother that we would explore other options when we got home that evening.

The tremendous weight of decision-making for Mother's future drained both Sandy and me. We needed each other to maintain a balance . . . a balance that was becoming more fragile with each passing day.

2

God, My World Is Caving In

*Their sorrows shall be multiplied that
hasten after another god
(Psalm 16:4a).*

Time was slipping by too quickly, and I felt I'd never catch up with it.

Mother's affliction seemed to have turned my whole life upside down, changing its course so completely that all I wanted to do was escape. I wanted something, anything, to block out all the guilt and hurt that haunted me. I needed something to numb the pain, to put me into "slow motion," and to help me sleep well at night.

Sandy and I shared a kinship that was rare among sisters . . . we knew it and we reveled in it. We were the best of friends.

In times of personal difficulties, we had the ability to filter thoughts through each other and we acted as buffers against tides of adversity. During complicated times, we could pour out our hearts knowing that each had the compassion it took to dispel the other's worry or anxiety. We carried one another's burdens using the tools of love and a warm, trusting relationship that had been nurtured since childhood. Clearly we helped each other weave the fabric of our individual lives.

This time, however, our burdens were mutual and we found it not only complicated but awkward as we tried to carry this gigantic weight. Instead of Mother's condition having a unifying impact on our lives, I felt as though it was destroying us.

The evening after our visit with Mother, Sandy and I talked well into the night about the possible alternatives. We became convinced that as much as we felt it was our duty to take care of Mother, we were both emotionally taxed from the strain. Distressed by Mother's unrelenting religious convictions which constantly overrode our own meager beliefs, we concluded we were headed down a desperate road to nowhere.

Before I returned home, Sandy and I came to the conclusion that Mother would be better off in another nursing home. After making numerous phone calls, we chose one and her name was placed on a waiting list.

When we told Mother about the decision,

she brimmed with confidence, truly believing that this move would be a step forward and it would be the place where "science" would perform the miracle she'd been assuring us would transpire.

According to her beliefs, she hadn't experienced a healing because her thinking was confused. Mother's theory implied that the root of her disease, which she referred to as "illusion," was a fundamental error in her thinking. She attempted to clarify her thoughts through years of studying the Christian Science textbook *Science and Health with Key to the Scriptures,* reading the Bible, and praying. When her thoughts ultimately became clear, she believed, she would be healed. Then she would boldly thank God and give much gratitude to Mary Baker Eddy, the founder of Christian Science.

I found it difficult to understand why Mother, who had dedicated over twenty years to her religion, was unable to claim a healing. She trusted God implicitly, was faithful to her beliefs, and was secure in the continuous prayers of her practitioners.

She worked very hard at her religion and yet her efforts seemed to be in vain. Was this justice? I became harrowed with her illness and the needless suffering. I was even more angry at God for allowing this devastating thing to happen to her. How could he return her love in such a way?

There were times when I'd been informed by other Christian Scientists that my thinking could prevent Mother's healing. I was forced to live under her spiritual shadow. But I often thought what a curious shadow it was; one of despair and sadness, and so utterly self-willed. Darkened by confusion, I was slipping into apathetic indifference toward Mother's illness. After all, if Mother didn't want medical treatment, why should I be so concerned? I was unable to deal with the boundaries and perimeters Mother had placed around herself. My good judgment was continuously being questioned, creating a cloud of inadequacy that hovered over me. Interaction between Mother and me was tremendously one-sided, sometimes generating tension and strain.

Finally, one clear morning in September, we gathered Mother's belongings and headed toward another new home. My Uncle Russ and Aunt Helen, Mother's brother and sister-in-law, who'd been a constant source of encouragement to us, came along for the ride. They helped make the trip bearable. Uncle Russ used his marvelous sense of humor to amuse Mother, relaxing her into laughter. He had a way of calming us all. Still, it was a joyless way to celebrate Mother's sixty-first birthday!

Even though the new nursing home was just an hour from my house, the ride seemed interminable. But when we reached the home and drove through the beautiful grounds amid a lush, rolling countryside, I was pleasantly surprised and my mood was uplifted. My initial impression was very positive. Already I knew it was far superior to the previous nursing home. The facilities were fastidiously maintained—modern and clean.

We were met at our car by a polite young nurse who brought a wheelchair for Mother's convenience. This was a first for Mother. Up until then she'd refused any such help.

Once we got inside, I was even more impressed. We were taken down a wide, softly carpeted, cheerful corridor to Mother's room which was spacious and attractively furnished. One wall encompassed a glass window overlooking some of the gardens. It was artistically decorated with pretty drapes and delicate yellow carpeting. It was warm and appealing, much more suited to Mother's taste and a welcome change from the cold, bare linoleum of the other home.

"This is more like it, Mother!" I said, eagerly chatting about how nice everything was while I opened the drapes to check the view.

"You'll be much happier here. I just know you will!" I said, refusing to look at her for a response. Instead I helped the nurse get her settled and then busied myself unpacking and testing the radio and television. At first she seemed pleased and I think her hopes soared momentarily.

However, as darkness set in and it was time to leave, Mother indicated her displeasure. I had seen it coming all day but had refused to acknowledge it. When she expressed her discontent by asking me to take her home, I became very annoyed with her. After all the arrangements we'd made, the driving we'd done, the packing and unpacking again, I couldn't believe she'd express any dissatisfaction!

"Now, Mother," I said, restraining myself. "I want you to give this some time. When you get better, we'll bring you home, OK?"

She gave no response. But the hurt of rejecting her pierced my heart. *O God!* I thought. *Where are you? How much more of this are you going to allow her to take?*

When we finally left we were all crying. I felt as though I'd abandoned her again.

Day by day the pressure within me continued to build, releasing an emotional tug-of-war. Every week, for two solid months, Mother begged me to take her out. Each time I refused. By Thanksgiving she'd given up asking and I saw increasing signs of spiritual defeat. Where was her healing? Where was her God? Had he forgotten her?

The promise that I'd bring her home for

Christmas gave her something to look forward to and helped me deal with my conscience.

When Ted and I arrived at the nursing home on Christmas Eve, Mother was eagerly waiting for us. We gently lifted her onto the front seat of the car. She had lost twenty-five pounds in three months and looked like a skeleton. She was in tremendous pain, so we had to be extremely careful how we touched her. I was hesitant to add additional pressure from the seat belt, so I slipped into the back seat and gently wrapped my arms around her to keep her from wobbling from side to side. It was a long, arduous drive home.

When we arrived, we covered Mother with blankets as protection against the cold, then Ted tenderly carried her into the house. We settled her comfortably into her favorite reclining chair in the den. I felt exhausted.

Besides trying to prepare a huge Christmas dinner, wrapping presents, and doing last-minute decorating, I became Mother's full-time nurse. She no longer walked, and lifting a spoon to her mouth was too difficult. The job was enormous! Ted and I and the three children took turns sitting with her, fearful of leaving her alone for any length of time.

Somehow, though, the joy outweighed the sorrow as one by one the rest of the family came to our house for the Christmas festivities. Sandy and her family arrived along with my twenty-one-year-old brother. Mother was overjoyed with all the holiday excitement. Being surrounded by her entire family made her stay complete.

By Christmas afternoon Mother was experiencing excruciating pain. She asked me to phone her practitioner.

Throughout her illness Mother had had constant support and advice from one practitioner or another. We encouraged this because we felt that it was a source of comfort to her. Since Mother was unable to speak, I was responsible for making the calls. They were supposed to be progress reports, yet there rarely was progress. Our monthly bills from the practitioners often exceeded our expectations.

Many times I'd wished that I could think, feel, and react the way Mother did in order that I might understand her better. But it was difficult to do. Our invisible wall was growing stronger and higher, and I discovered that I was incapable of breaking it down.

Instead of Mother's pain diminishing, it worsened as the hours passed. Since talking with the practitioner, she appeared more defeated than she had at any other time since we'd brought her home.

I suggested that I get her settled in bed for a little while, hoping that the relaxation would ease the pain. Getting Mother comfortable was no easy task. It took at least a half hour before

I got her into a position that suited her.

Whenever Mother wasn't seeing progress, she would replace one practitioner with another. Today was no exception. Upon her suggestion, I phoned someone else, explaining Mother's condition. I'd told the story so many times to innumerable practitioners that I was weary of the repetition.

By eight o'clock Christmas night, it was time to take Mother back to the nursing home. All day she had made attempts to persuade me otherwise by writing notes that read: "You'll never know how grateful I am to be here." She wrote that the black recliner was the only chair on earth that gave her comfort. When I promised to buy her one for her room, her disappointment was obvious and tore at my heart again. I reasoned that if we shared the same house, the love that we had for each other would be sorely tried. My relationship with Ted and my three children would suffer, and I was afraid to take that chance. I felt the demands she would make on my time would consume me.

Because of the guilt that I felt, I became a very unhappy person. Lacking control in many areas of my life, I began to enclose myself in self-pity. I felt as though I was sliding quickly into a depression and was terrified that I'd never come out of it. I needed help, but didn't know how to go about getting it. I doubted that there was anyone in the world who had any answers for me. I became irritable and lazy. Everything was an effort. My attitude strongly affected my relationship with Ted and our children, but I was unable to change it.

My standards were extremely high. I demanded perfection from myself as well as from Ted and the children. They were failing to meet my requirements and I was unsuccessful in meeting my self-imposed pattern for living.

Because Ted was such a good provider, I was surrounded with material things. I should have been satisfied with my life, but instead a disturbance festered within me. Life was growing void of meaning or purpose.

Preferring to bury my emotions, I began to lead a long, lonely struggle against self-destruction. During the months that followed, I stumbled through like a robot.

There were days when I barely had enough energy to brush my teeth. Keeping the house looking neat and pretty was a struggle, but I'd push myself because it was important to me to have things in order. To me, sloppiness revealed a lack of discipline. Often I'd compliment myself on my ability to rearrange the furniture, make cute curtains, redecorate a room, and always know just the spot for the little accent piece that I "had to have." Each time I'd pass that spot I'd admire it; but I always thought it peculiar when, as time wore on, I'd barely notice it anymore. How soon the thrill and pleasure would fade. Everything was so temporary . . . nothing lasted!

Deep down there was trouble in my mind and body and no one to extricate it. I was in a terrifying spiral of depression, teetering on the brink of a nervous breakdown . . . building up fear of the unknown and feeling as though my world was caving in. All because I felt responsible for a situation I couldn't physically or mentally manage.

3

Someone to Listen

*In the day when I cried thou
answeredst me, and strengthenedst
me with strength in my soul
(Psalm 138:3).*

My sister recognized my need and wanted to
help. She tried in various ways, but somehow
the chasm in my life wasn't being filled by anyone or anything. Although I knew Sandy
would be able to understand the depression
that closed in around me, even her suggestions
seemed inadequate.

One day, looking at me in concern, she said,
"Bonnie, you really need to have a friend to
share your thoughts. You're so close to Toni,
why don't you confide in her?"

"No friend of mine is going to know all that's
happening inside of me," I said. "Besides, we
have a good friendship and I'm not going to
turn it into a pity party."

"Who says you have to bare your soul? Just
find someone who can understand and help

you through this time. Women have a way of helping other women."

I mentally refused the suggestion and continued to carry the load alone, dragging myself through each day.

Then one day Tim, a very dear friend of ours, arrived with the dreadful news that his best friend had committed suicide. He was full of questions about God and heaven, looking for answers to why something like this had happened.

Though I desperately wanted to help Tim, I didn't have the answers. I believed in God and went to church, but no words of comfort came to me. I was numb. The only thing I could do was listen to him, but that wasn't enough and I knew it.

When Tim left I felt a cold, dark emptiness settle over me. Wasn't there an answer anywhere for those of us who weren't coping?

I ran to the phone and called Toni. She was the only friend I knew who seemed to have her life in order.

"Toni, you have to help me!" I said.

"I'll be happy to; what can I do?"

"Well, Tim was just here and . . . Toni, I didn't have any answers for him. I told him that I was going to talk to you because I knew that you would write to him. You will, won't you? You have such a beautiful way with words and, quite frankly, I'm at a total loss."

A few days later Toni handed me a copy of the letter she had sent Tim.

"Take it home and read it. It makes me uncomfortable to have you read it now," she said, a little embarrassed.

It was a good letter. Everything about it was comforting; but she talked about having a relationship with Jesus Christ and I really wished she had eliminated that part. Tim would probably think that she'd become a religious fanatic, and I didn't want him to be offended at such a critical time.

When Toni asked me what I thought about the letter, I lied a little and told her it was wonderful. After all, how do you tell somebody that she should have deleted the part about Jesus? Obviously, she was sincere, and I didn't want to hurt her.

Tim, however, liked the letter, and that was the most important thing. It helped him get through some difficult days, and I felt it certainly was better than anything I had been able to say.

Still, the mere fact that I was unable to reach Tim with hope had crippled me with grief. Turning the problem over to Toni didn't cure my need to help. I couldn't see how religion could satisfy the emptiness that Tim was experiencing. Was religion helping Mother? What was the remedy? There seemed to be none.

That winter Ted and I vacationed in the British West Indies and stayed on the island of Tobago. It was a wonderful respite, but things continued to slide downward emotionally for me. I had always had difficulty coming down off the mountaintop after a vacation; post-vacation blues generally dominated me for several days. This time, a few days grew into weeks, and I became alarmed.

Wasted hours and days were spent lying in bed, sleeping. Sad music enhanced my gray moods, creating a sense of total loss. Convinced I was incapable of being the kind of person I wanted to be, I withdrew more and more.

I read numerous articles on depression which were frightening. Words of desperation were printed on each page and rarely was there a ray of hope written in the heavy-hearted paragraphs. Yet I was drawn to them repeatedly. I related to every article so much that I began to imagine what had happened in the magazine stories was, in fact, happening to me. I could have convinced myself of anything!

The suicide of Tim's friend confirmed for me the end result of too much depression. Yet I kept wondering what was going on, and if this could happen to me.

Hiding from reality, I entangled myself in a web of desperate fear. It was spring, yet to me it seemed like the dead of winter.

My imagination, constantly working overtime, convinced me that I was going to become another statistic. Nothing helped, and Mother's lingering illness, her absolute dependence on me, and the mounting bills at the nursing home made everything worse.

Around Christmastime my brother Charley came from the West Coast for an extended visit. Fourteen years separated us, and my mothering tendency toward him was strong. He was like my own child, yet I never wanted to assume responsibility for him. As a self-reliant person, he didn't expect it. He had left home after high school graduation, returning infrequently.

Charley had rejected Mother's beliefs when he became a teenager, stubbornly refusing to attend church with her. Because he was independent and spontaneous, we looked upon his decision as a blatant act of disrespect.

I would rarely permit myself to see from Charley's vantage point. He was a product of the "sixties generation" and I had little in common with him. Yet there remained a thread of kinship that held us together.

When Charley came home he arrived without a car, with little money, and no job. Since Mother now lived in a nursing facility, he had no home. He brought along a dog who was his constant companion and treasured friend.

Recognizing that I had too many problems of my own, he sought refuge with our cousins. They welcomed Charley and their generosity removed a load of guilt from my shoulders. Yet, just enough guilt still lingered to drag me even further down. Would there ever be an end to all this responsibility?

No matter how well-intentioned I was, or how much I wanted to help my brother, I became virtually handicapped, emotionally and spiritually.

One morning while Charley was home, we sat for hours discussing Mother and the ordeal involved. He recalled painful memories from his childhood.

During our conversation, Charley and I recognized that our past was unchangeable; we were stuck with the effect it had on us. Both our lives were profoundly influenced by the strength of Mother's convictions. We knew we could learn from the experience, but we could never escape it. Our past was an integral component of our being. That day I learned a lesson in compassion by feeling Charley's hurts and respecting his individuality.

When he left, I watched at the kitchen window as he walked toward the street. His dog followed close at his heels, and Charley lovingly patted his head and called his name. All I could see was my kid brother who needed a new pair of pants, a good haircut, a home, and a mother—none of which he had. The only thing in life he could really call his own was a dog. How I ached to make up for the past and meet all his needs. Tears streamed down my cheeks as he turned to wave good-bye.

The following morning Charley found his dog along the side of the road, dead. He'd been poisoned.

Where were the answers to life and its complexities? Surely I hadn't found any. Sadly, I didn't know anyone that had.

The following weeks and months crawled by and my depression deepened. I just wished that one morning I'd awaken and this whole mess would be gone, over at last.

The air was heavy with humidity and the sun was hidden beneath thick gray clouds. The weather was a picture of my mood, a condition I'd grown accustomed to over the past four years. The depression had besieged me much too long.

I was straightening up the house, still wearing my robe, eager to slip back into bed when Toni called to ask if she could come over for a cup of coffee. Before I knew it, I'd committed myself.

Toni had been my friend for a long time. She and her husband had a solid relationship, more stable than many other couples that we knew. I admired their marriage and life-style.

I'd noticed, however, that their lives had begun to change recently. There seemed to be a deepening in their faith. Every time I visited their home I noticed a Bible opened on the den table. It was obvious that someone in the family had taken an interest in it. I kept my distance by refusing to ask any questions. One thing I knew for sure, I didn't need any more religion in my life!

I recalled a recent conversation with Toni.

"Bonnie," she'd said. "Don asked me if I really knew what a Christian was." I couldn't imagine why Toni's husband would ask her such a question and was somewhat amused and intrigued by their exchange of words. After all, she was an exemplary Christian. Anyone who was as nice as she was and went to church as often as she did certainly knew what it meant to be a Christian.

Then Toni looked at me and asked, "What do you think a Christian is?"

Having never thought too much about it, I simply said, "Well, a Christian is a person who . . . well, he believes in God and goes to church regularly. Generally, he is a kind, good person." I wasn't too confident about what I'd said but it was the best answer I could give. I sincerely believed that one could just be an American citizen and be considered a Christian. Church really had nothing to do with it.

Toni understood what I meant, but said that

Don took the definition even further by explaining that a Christian had to have a personal relationship with Jesus Christ, making him Lord and Savior of his life. Such words sounded prejudiced and pious to me. I'd never in my whole life heard such a statement.

To me, Jesus was just a person from the Bible, a book I seldom read because it was too difficult to understand. After all, Jesus was dead, wasn't he? Hadn't he died hanging on a cross? Wasn't that what Good Friday and Easter were all about?

I didn't ask Toni those questions for fear she'd see my ignorance if I was wrong. I really knew very little about the Bible even though I had been reared in a "religious" home.

Now, as I waited for Toni to come over for coffee, I pondered my relationship with her. I remembered Sandy's advice about talking with Toni. Yet there remained within me a stubborn battle with pride, pride that kept me from admitting to anyone all my inner turmoil and depression. I'd be able to work it out eventually, wouldn't I?

Still, Toni was my friend. Surely I could trust her. So I made a decision: if Toni came over before ten o'clock, I'd discuss some things with her. If she didn't, I'd hurry, get dressed, and play the little game I'd gotten so adept at playing: the game of pretending everything was all right.

At five minutes to ten Toni walked in. I looked wretched and felt the same way. Her sympathetic expression caused the tension within me to ease. In the midst of my shuffling emotions a wave of confusion rolled over me causing a flood of tears. I sat numbly, surrounded by flashes of doubt and wondering if I would ever recover. Without a moment's hesitation I began to sob, crying out to be understood. Then I began to open up and suddenly became myself for the first time in ages.

The hurt and tears overwhelmed Toni, too. As only one who is capable of understanding could do, my friend cried along with me. She sensed a need for my frustration to be addressed immediately.

Her mature sensitivity and the tenacious allegiance to her faith in God brought a sense of calm to the surface. "Bonnie, I'm really sorry. I wish I could help, but I honestly don't know how." She hesitated, took a deep breath, then said, "I know someone who can though."

"Really? Who?" I asked, thinking she must know a good counselor.

"Jesus," she said.

Ordinarily, a statement like that would have irritated me, but strangely, this time it didn't.

With that, Toni fumbled through her purse until she found two little gold-colored booklets entitled, "Have You Heard of the Four Spiritual Laws?" When she handed me one she asked if I'd ever seen it before.

"No," I replied.

I sat, listening pensively and following along in my copy of the pamphlet as Toni read hers aloud, telling me that God loved me, that he offered a wonderful plan for my life, but that through sin I had become separated from this loving God. As she continued to read I was struck with the truth of my sin, and listened even more intently as she came to the section about Christ being God's only provision for our sins. Finally I began to understand the reality of who Christ was, and what he meant to me in my life. I began to see that I *could* get out of the darkness into which I seemed to be falling, but only with Christ's help.

When Toni reached the section that showed the difference between a self-directed life and a Christ-directed life, there was no doubt which one represented me . . . the self-directed life of discord and frustration had been mine for years. Yet, when we came to the end and the pamphlet asked if the concluding prayer inviting Jesus into my life expressed the desire of my heart, I hesitated.

Did it really express the desire of my heart? I wasn't certain. To be perfectly honest, I wasn't convinced I truly understood the meaning of the prayer.

Toni asked me if I wanted to pray. Her eyes beckoned me to admit a need that I wasn't sure my heart was ready to recognize.

"I'd feel a little funny doing that right here in the kitchen," I told her, hoping she would understand. "I'll pray later, OK?"

She respected my wishes and didn't press me or make me feel uncomfortable about my decision to hold back. We talked for a while longer, but it wasn't until after she had gone that I realized something had happened to me. I couldn't explain it, but it was as though a tremendous weight had been lifted from my shoulders. In the midst of my chaotic circumstances, I felt a new balance and a hope, as well as a sense of tranquillity.

When Ted and I went to bed that night, I was wide awake. After about fifteen minutes of tossing and turning, I slipped out quietly and walked down the hallway through the kitchen and into the den. There on the table sat the little gold pamphlet. I picked it up and reread the prayer at the end.

> Lord Jesus, I need you. Thank you for dying on the cross for my sins. I open the door of my life and receive you as my Savior and Lord. Thank you for forgiving my sins and giving me eternal life. Take control of the throne of my life. Make me the kind of person you want me to be.

I read the prayer over and over again. What was it *really* saying?

"God, if you're actually up there," I said in a hushed tone, "please show me what you want me to know."

I glanced down at the prayer again. The last sentence appeared strangely different. The "you" looked like it was larger than any other word, as though it was coming right off the page.

Suddenly everything began to make sense. God desired to change me and make me the kind of person *he* wanted.

There was something about God's love and his plan that caused me to pray. At once a calm, strengthening peace enveloped me, and to this day it has never left.

I certainly didn't understand what had happened, but I was sure of one thing—I could not have continued the way I'd been living. That night I slept soundly, awakening the next morning to a brilliantly gorgeous day. I felt as beautiful as the weather.

"I don't understand what has happened to me," I said, "I just know I'm not the same person . . . please let it last. Oh, God, I really, really hope it lasts!"

4

A Room for Mother

But if any provide not for his own,
and specially for those of his own
house, he hath denied the faith,
and is worse than an infidel
(1 Timothy 5:8).

Just as I'd felt the beauty and warmth of the June day running through my veins, I realized that the frightening depressive spiral that had controlled me for so long had suddenly and unexpectedly vanished. Gone were those dark dreary days. I truly had never expected to recover, so I was amazed at how alive I felt, so eager to make up for lost time. Those dead months . . . those wasted hours . . . could I ever recapture them?

I pinched myself every so often, wondering if my feelings were real. The inevitable doubts occurred. "Surely this could never last; the depression will return." But life began to take on new meaning so rapidly that it almost became a blur of frantic activity. Overnight it seemed that the fog of apathy finally had lifted.

I wondered how I would ever find the time to accomplish all there was to be done.

During the month of May, I had been forced to move Mother to another nursing home. The basic weekly fee from the previous home had escalated far beyond what Mother's income permitted. The unexpected move caused increased apprehension and I knew Mother had been unhappy from the moment she arrived.

Before admitting her, I'd explained Mother's religious convictions to both the administrator and the head nurse. They promised to respect them. However, I knew it wouldn't be easy for anyone.

Mother's days and nights were frightening as she lay in agonizing pain. The nurses were unable to give her the constant attention she felt she deserved. I'd grown accustomed to her persistent grumbling. Now, instead of once a week, I found myself visiting her daily, trying to smooth over some of the problems. I thought it helped when I was there, but she continued to write volumes of notes lamenting the treatment.

There were many days I didn't want to visit Mother because I felt guilty and was simply unable to handle her complaints. One day, after she had been there about a month, as soon as I walked into the room she handed me her little white tablet scrawled with words.

I gazed into her face; it was drawn by fear and sadness, expectant of rejection, and it made my emotions even more intense.

Looking back at the note clutched in my hand, I reread the scribbled message. "Take me home, even if you stick me in the attic. Quite an experience last nite." Immediately I mentally considered the complications of this request. Because of my obligations to my husband and children, I deemed the proposal outrageous. Yet this time I knew I could no longer ignore or brush aside her request.

"Oh, God," I prayed, "what am I going to do with this enormous problem?"

I was conscious of Mother staring at me. Sensing she wanted an immediate answer, I avoided her eyes as long as possible.

When I finally looked her way, I noticed her gorgeous eyes were dimmed with sadness and emptiness. My heart ached with grief. She was a tormented woman, void of contentment and peace. I was suddenly consumed with the painful realization of what might lie ahead.

"Mother," I said gently, "why do you want me to take you home?" She nodded for her writing pad and pen.

Over the past nine months she had become very weak and experienced extreme difficulty as she wrote. Her little hands could no longer hold the pad, so I held it for her as she struggled to write. As always, her desire to communicate was incredibly strong. To her it was always worth the effort.

Arduously, she described the horrible incident that had happened the night before. My eyes widened in shock as I followed the marks of her pen. The night nurse had become so irritated with her that she had barged into the room, grabbed Mother by her head, and thrown her up against the pillow.

With a heavy heart, I began to picture the scene in my mind. Isolated and lonely, she lay in bed, a motionless body besieged with pain, unable to change positions for relief. Inwardly, she was screaming for help and no one really cared.

The room was dark and chilly, the shades drawn tightly, the door securely shut despite repeated requests to keep it ajar. Mother panicked as darkness enveloped her room. She didn't have enough strength to press the nurses' bell. There was no choice but to cry out for their attention.

Mother then wrote pages of notes describing the treatment she'd been receiving from one night nurse who excused her actions by telling Mother that she disturbed the other patients when she whined so loudly.

While Mother wrote, I thought of the many patients who would have been just like her if they had not been sedated right after dinner. Because Mother refused this, she was accused of creating havoc.

One of her messages read, "Thought I'd gone the other nite under the pounding of my body." She wrote how she could feel her "bones crack" when the nurse "threw her around." Even though the nurse is very rough, she "appears otherwise in front of others. With another nurse helping, she becomes kind." The night nurse even refused to call Mother's practitioner.

We were entangled in a battle of wills. Mother was unalterable in her convictions; the nurses were immovable in theirs. It was easy for me to see how this could happen, but hard for me to understand the barrage of physical abuse Mother was forced to endure from a woman trained to care for the sick. If things were that bad, I should have been called in to discuss the matter. I was certain no one else was aware of what had transpired.

Questions raced through my mind. I wondered if Mother had made a habit of calling for help too frequently. Maybe the nurse was angry because she refused medication. Nevertheless, I could find no justification for the nurse's unethical behavior.

I felt an urge to storm the nurses' station, but Mother's immediate comfort was more important than my raging frustration. Endeavoring to find the right words to soothe her, I silently prayed, "Please, God, help me know what to do."

As Mother looked into my eyes I could see her searching for security in me, security I felt I couldn't provide. Unconsciously, I stood on the threshold of a complete role reversal, something neither of us was prepared to handle. Possibly it might be easier for me to accept than for Mother. She might resent the changes no matter how much she understood the rationale behind them.

I took Mother's frail little face gently between my hands and smoothed away her tears. I thought of how precious her face was; kindness had never left it. I couldn't control the tears that welled up in my own eyes and spilled down my flushed cheeks.

With a warm heart and a quiet voice, I said, "Mother, you know I can't make a decision like this without the family, don't you?" She nodded in agreement. "I'm going home to talk to Ted and the children and I'll be back tonight." Her eyes smiled at me. "I love you, Mother," I said, replacing her head on the pillow and tenderly tucking the covers around her delicate body. Kissing her cheek softly, I turned and walked out the door. I knew that those few short words of hope had lifted her heart as they had mine.

As I strode along the gloomy corridor, a

surprising sense of peace swept over me. I walked straight out of the entrance and into my car. The urge to confront the nurses had vanished.

Driving home, I reflected on Mother's note. How would my recent decision of accepting Christ into my life affect my response? What if my family didn't want my mother to live with us?

Whatever the disease was that plagued Mother, it had now affected her arms and legs, and especially her speech, swallowing, and breathing. Her head slumped forward continuously, causing discomfort in her neck. Dressing had become increasingly difficult and we had resorted to pull-on clothing. Even that, after a while, became complicated. She refused a cane. A walker was a last resort. Her needs were constantly escalating.

Yet, despite the physical battle, Mother fought the progressive immobilization. As much as possible, she lived her life as though nothing was wrong. Her absence of self-pity and her dedication were commendable qualities.

Never did she show any visible signs of a lack of confidence, a sense of being deprived, or any outward despair or panic. Mother had no doubt that she would be healed. Her mind remained extremely sharp.

While I never would have wanted Mother to be obsessed with her illness, I knew she had not reconciled herself to her present condition. She refused to accept the advancing degeneration.

She had always been full of self-confidence, but the suffering and slow deterioration of these past five years had left her more compliant.

Also, our relationship had suffered. We just hadn't seen eye to eye. Mother was strong-willed and stubborn. I guess I was too. As I thought about these things, something stirred within me. Unexpectedly, I felt a protective love for her, the type of love I remembered in my childhood when we shared a rich, close rapport. I knew the time had come to seriously consider her requests to come home.

At dinner, Ted and the children listened attentively as I unfolded the day's events. Without a moment's reservation the children said that their grandmother should come to live with us. Ted was more cautious, concerned about me and the pressure of Mother's care. I understood his apprehension.

I knew he wasn't sold on the idea of his invalid mother-in-law moving into our home. I wanted him to say yes and yet I was afraid of a positive response. How in the world could I ever do the job? Still, I tried to convince Ted that it *could* be done, and with each persuasive word to him, I assured myself.

I faced the questions running through my mind: What was this going to do to our lives? I hadn't even begun to achieve a sufficient balance in my own life; how could I consider an enormous undertaking like this? Could this ruin my marriage? Was I prepared to risk that? Was I really ready to have my whole life turned upside down? I knew the answers were no.

But when I balanced these objections against the resident doctor's prognosis, "She only has three weeks," I told myself she had to come home. If I couldn't turn from my own needs for a short while to help Mother with hers, I'd feel guilty for the rest of my life. I also knew I could never recapture this period once it was gone.

She would need round-the-clock attention, twenty-four-hour care. How could it be done? Endless questions emerged only to be answered, once again, by the doctor's prognosis.

I wanted Ted to act and respond decisively, to give me a definite yes or no. More than that, I wanted to be able to accept his decision wholeheartedly, whatever it was. He seemed noncommittal and reserved. I was having difficulty seeing things from his perspective.

How could Ted completely understand? He hadn't been with me when I watched my grief-stricken mother begging for help, stretching out her hand to be rescued. He couldn't possibly imagine the melancholy, dreary air that had hung in Mother's room today, because he hadn't been there. How could I expect this of him? Still, I held him responsible for not feeling all that I felt. There lay between us more anxiety than I ever wanted to admit.

My heart grew cold as I discovered I was grieving, grieving for the inevitable death of a parent and because I sensed that I was carrying this burden all alone. Walls began to grow around me as I pulled the sorrow closer to me, embracing it in loneliness and self-pity.

It was obvious that I was to be the one to make the final decision. Before the day was over, I contacted Toni, who asked me to open my Bible and read 1 Timothy 5:8: "But if any provide not for his own and specially for those of his own house, he hath denied the faith, and is worse than an infidel."

I was amazed that words like that were in the Bible. I'd never understood anything in the Bible before, but these words seemed so clear—as though they'd been placed there just for me to read. I was fascinated that they struck me the way they did.

"Toni, do you think this is a sign that I should bring Mother home?" I asked.

"This is the way God speaks to us," she said.

Having God speak to me in *any* way was

new. However, I had an innocent trust that what I had just read should be followed and that God wanted me to bring Mother home to care for her. I was sure that God knew where my strength was going to come from. Intuitively, I felt that he wouldn't allow my marriage to fail if I did what he wanted me to do.

As promised, I returned to the nursing home that night. Before entering Mother's room, I consulted with the nurses. They assured me that the attending physician had said she had about three more weeks to live. By this time she had refused regular food and was taking only the supplements. Any good daughter, I thought, would give her mother three weeks.

I realized for the first time that I had to recognize and deal with the indisputable reality of Mother's affliction, something I'd required of her long ago and yet had never expected of myself. Actually, up until that time, I thought I *had* accepted it.

When I entered the room that night, Mother appeared relieved, looking at me as though she'd been counting the minutes until my return. I wondered if she had thought I might not come back. Her eyes looked hopeful. I told her the good news first.

"We're going to bring you home, Mother," I said with as much enthusiasm as I could muster. "The kids are thrilled. Are you happy?"

Her face was a blaze of color and a laugh came from her throat. She desperately wanted to express herself, but couldn't; yet I understood without a word. It's funny how contagious joy is. The room seemed filled with a bright anticipation.

Then I sat down and explained that we had intended to leave for vacation in a couple of days. I told Mother that the plans had been made for a long time and that we didn't want to disappoint the children.

The smile never left Mother's face. Not even that news could dampen her spirits.

"I'll call every night to check on you and I'll be back on Wednesday to see you." Her smile remained.

"Now, I want you to try with all your strength not to call for the night nurse. Do you think that you will be able to do that?"

She nodded.

"Also, why don't you ask your practitioner to pray a little harder and I will too."

She nodded her head again.

The calm that I felt seemed reflected on Mother's face as well, and when I left her she was relaxed and curiously resigned. Seeds of hope had been planted in her, and I felt them growing in me as well.

That night I didn't realize what lay ahead, where the God I was beginning to trust would lead us. Yet I was at peace. Little did I know that my words were a commitment for the next four years of our lives.

Our week of vacation at the shore was the most relaxing time I'd ever remembered. Something unusual was happening within me, something I was unable to define. It was wonderful and I wanted it to last forever. That week I read my first Christian book, *Tramp for the Lord,* by Corrie ten Boom. It amazed me how such a little woman could trust God with everything. I convinced myself as I read that faith like hers was for super Christians . . . only special people enjoyed that kind of relationship with God.

While on vacation Ted had become disturbingly quiet and reserved every time I mentioned Mother's situation. Fearful of the permanency of her stay, and wary of the demands on my time, he was projecting far ahead of me. His uncertainty was playing perilously with my emotions.

The situation was causing silence to grow between us. I was sure it would worsen before it would improve. Ted seemed afraid of the consequences, yet he didn't feel free to say no. I knew he really wanted to understand, but was struggling with the situation all the same. Surprisingly, I had unusual patience for his reticence.

My sister, who had arrived for a visit, was

waiting for me when we returned from vacation. "Mother is waiting to be brought home tomorrow," she said. Suddenly I was hit with the reality of our decision. I wasn't prepared for my reaction.

"Well, I'm just not ready to bring her home tomorrow. Ted's having second thoughts and we have things to iron out and I won't bring her home until they're settled!" I felt trapped, torn between a commitment to Mother and Ted's indecisiveness.

The following day as Sandy was leaving, one of my cousins stopped by. We all decided to go out for breakfast.

At the restaurant, we discussed how I was going to handle the problem. Suddenly I said, "Let's go to the store. I want to buy Mother a new electric toothbrush, and pretty towels and flowery sheets for her bed."

I shopped like a mother preparing for her child's birthday. Never had I been so impulsive. How ridiculous, I thought. There wasn't even a bed for the sheets!

That night I asked Ted to try to come to grips with the problem we faced because I needed a definite answer.

His response was cool. "I won't stand in your way."

"Ted, I know that you have some anxieties about Mother moving in," I said quietly. "It's only natural for you to be a bit anxious. Perhaps if I plan carefully I'll be able to alleviate most of your concerns.

"Listen to some of my ideas: Mother can afford some outside help, and I've already had someone offer to help on Sunday mornings so that we can start to attend church more regularly. I'm planning to put an ad in the local paper and we'll wait to see what happens from that.

"I have to rent a hospital bed and other equipment, and call an ambulance to bring Mother home on Wednesday.

"All we can do is try. If it doesn't work, we'll make other plans. Please be patient and give me enough time to work things out. I'll do everything I can to make it run smoothly, with as little interruption to our normal routine as possible."

I so desperately wanted Ted to put his arms around me and say, "OK, Honey, we'll give it a try." But he was just too unsure.

The next day I contacted an old high school friend named Carole and asked her if she would help me with Mother's care. She agreed to give it a try. Since she wasn't a stranger to Mother, I felt they would get along. Besides, Carole had been a close friend for almost twenty-five years, so we would be free to be ourselves. Throughout those years we had maintained a mutual respect and love for one another. She was willing to learn all she needed to know to care for Mother, and I was excited about teaching her.

I then got in touch with the local emergency squad and arranged to bring Mother home. After that, I ordered a hospital bed from a rental company, and the kids and I got busy preparing her room.

We had recently added a small guest room with a full bath onto our home, so we began arranging Mother's belongings there. We worked to create a quiet, restful environment, and hung her favorite pictures on the paneled walls. We made it as comfortable as possible, using colorful sheets on the bed to add a touch of spring. By the time we were finished, it looked homey and pleasant. We knew "Nanna" would be pleased. Our day was brightened just from the effort.

The next two days were a flurry of activity. There was much to do to prepare for Mother's homecoming. It was June 29, 1977.

By the time my youngest child, Brooke, and I arrived at the nursing home, the ambulance was waiting. I shivered knowing that it was the vehicle that would provide Mother's way home. I had talked to Brooke about riding with "Nanna" in the ambulance to keep her company. She thought it was a super idea. Her self-confidence and the new adventure of riding in an ambulance outweighed any fears I might have had that the experience would frighten her.

The nurses stood by observing the unique event. I think that some of them were happy to see Mother go and others thought I must be crazy. One of them said, "No one has ever left here alive."

However, one nurse took my arm as the attendants wheeled Mother down the corridor and said softly, "She won't be around long, dear." I knew she meant well by her comment and I returned a smile, agreeing with her.

Mother was delighted that Brooke was riding with her, and her face was radiant as she was lifted into the ambulance. She had a look of expectancy and the twinkle in her eyes went beyond our invisible barriers and straight to my heart.

There was a light air in my stride as I walked through the doors of the nursing home for the last time. I felt completely confident that what we were doing was right. I jumped into my car and sped away as the ambulance followed. Catching a glimpse of it in the rearview mirror, I couldn't help wondering what was happening inside.

Emotionally rejuvenated, I was extremely optimistic. I laughed to myself, knowing some people questioned my reasoning. Yet I felt good about everything.

Unexpectedly, tears rolled down my face. I knew they were tears of joy because I was convinced that what I'd done was what God wanted me to do.

That now familiar verse rang through my mind over and over again: "But if any provide not for his own and specially for those of his own house, he hath denied the faith, and is worse than an infidel" (1 Timothy 5:8).

When we arrived home, the attendants lifted Mother carefully and gently placed her on the bed in her cozy little room. We were extremely impressed with them and thrilled at how effortlessly the morning had passed. My hopes continued to grow.

The first day I taught Carole everything I knew about caring for Mother. Before she left for home that night, Mother had been fed and was sitting comfortably in her chair. Carole and I had worked well together, even though I sensed some apprehension because of the responsibility involved in attending to Mother's needs. We vowed to help each other until our confidence was secure, knowing we could be honest if the situation got unmanageable.

When Ted arrived home, dinner was waiting for him. My plans not to interrupt the normal flow of our family life had worked. I was very pleased! I couldn't believe how well everything had gone the first day. So much had been accomplished in such a short time.

Ted listened with surprise as I detailed the day's events. Mother was happy to see him when he peeked in to say hello. I smiled as I listened to him tell her that he was glad she'd arrived. I hoped he really meant what he said, but only time would tell. She was cheerful and blinked her eyes three times, indicating that she loved him. I stood in the background just watching, pleased to see the warm exchange.

Later that evening Toni came over to help me lift Mother onto the commode before I got her ready for bed. I had hesitated calling her to come, but I couldn't ask anyone in the family. Not yet, anyway.

Everything we did was a learning experience. I was as dependent upon others as Mother was on me.

Toni and another close friend, Carlee, were willing to drop whatever they were doing to help. They were acutely aware of the heavy responsibilities and the importance of making this situation work.

With no training whatsoever, Toni and Carlee became the support team that I initially needed. Their lives illustrated to our family an unselfish giving of time, a necessary ingredient to get me through the beginning months. Their husbands were supportive and compassionate as well, allowing them the freedom to come whenever I called. The combination of love, patience, and confidence brought me through many exasperating experiences.

When I got Mother comfortable that first night we talked about all of the arrangements that still had to be made. Carole would work five days a week from nine to five, and I would take over the responsibility until a night nurse would come in at midnight. However, I had been unsuccessful in hiring a nurse for every night of the week. I'd placed an ad in the local paper and was hoping for a quick response. I still needed nurses for the weekends, even though my cousin said she would help if I needed her.

Mother sensed it wasn't going to be easy for any of us, but she gave me the impression that she would cooperate.

"Mother, I'm concerned about Ted and the children and I need to spend as much time with them as possible, you know." She looked at me with understanding eyes.

The next words I said just spilled out of my mouth, astonishing me.

"There's something I need to tell you," I began, "and though I feel a little strange saying it, I must. Ted and the children come first in my life," I hesitated, ". . . then you. If ever I think having you here becomes too much, we're going to have to make other arrangements. Do you understand?" Afraid of offending her, I said it in the gentlest way I knew how.

Unruffled by my words, she nodded. I was surprised by the freedom with which I spoke and by the conviction in my voice, but I meant it out of respect and love for everyone. Never before had I said anything like that. Some of the things I was beginning to think and verbalize amazed me.

Kissing her good-night, I said, "Mother, I want you to know I'm happy that things worked out so well today."

Because there was no nurse on duty that first night, it was necessary for me to sleep in the den so I could hear Mother if she needed me. She called out for help continuously. I turned her from one side to the other at least a dozen times. My sleep was interrupted like never before; but surprisingly, I awoke the next morning refreshed and energetic.

As the days passed the nurses were hired and, for the most part, everyone worked out well. Carole adjusted to the demands of the job and Mother grew a little more content, but she still had terrible pain and a dreadful fear of dying.

In late August the night nurse was unable to come. Again I slept in the den. I listened to Mother's endless groaning and crying. The agony was driving her crazy, yet she continued to hold to her firm convictions of not taking medication.

At that time in my life, I believed that the only way Mother could ever be relieved of that hideous pain was to die. Even though a twinge of guilt stung me, I prayed that God would let her die that night. I had always been taught that God was loving. Certainly he wouldn't want Mother to linger, suffering like this day after day. I told God that it would be the perfect night. The children were away with friends, and selfishly, I wanted to spare them the agony of Mother's death.

The next time I checked her, I had the strangest feeling that I would find her dead. God had honored many of my prayers since I'd become a Christian, and he knew how sick Mother was.

However, when I walked in, she looked up at me, frightened and weary, but very much alive.

I realized that God *had* answered my prayer. It was as though he said, "I'm not ready to take your mother." Surprisingly, I wasn't disappointed.

5
A Glimmer of Hope

*Come unto me, all ye that labor and
are heavy laden, and I will give
you rest (Matthew 11:28).*

The most difficult thing for me to deal with
after bringing Mother home was the way she
rejected my advice. She covered her genuine
emotions by denying her illness. This caused
our communication gap to widen, making it
impossible for us to be ourselves.

She was bent on ignoring and avoiding the
subject of her sickness. By doing this she
thought her suffering would diminish. She refused the sensitivity and perception of anyone
who didn't believe the way she did. When I
watched her lie in bed just getting worse, I felt
brokenhearted. To me, this all could have been
prevented.

The biggest obstacle for Mother was to admit that she was in pain. She knew that I wanted her to take some medication to relieve it,
though I rarely mentioned the subject. It both-

ered me to ask her to do what was against her wishes, even though many family members thought I should insist.

Mother consulted her practitioner almost daily. Attentively, he brought Mother tapes and spent hours reading to her. He was a strong, compassionate person, yet he was just one of a host of other practitioners Mother had had since the onset of her illness.

Increasingly I struggled with Mother's beliefs. For years I'd accepted whatever was said, but now much of what I was learning troubled me.

One day I felt an urge to question the practitioner, so we sat alone in the living room.

"Steve, do you believe that God looks down upon Mother and sees a 'perfect spiritual child of God'? That he doesn't see her as a sick person, in need of him?"

He glanced over at me with a placid look and replied, "I believe that God sees your mother only as a 'perfect spiritual child of God.' He does not see her as sick or dying because he only sees perfection."

Somehow, I couldn't quite imagine that if God knew everything, as I believed he did, he would be blind to the sickness and suffering in Mother's life. I became convinced that Steve's job was to persuade Mother that she was neither sick nor dying.

"Right before Mother was taken from the

nursing home, I prayed for God to help me to make decisions. I really believe that he is able to see the whole picture, the bad as well as the good. He knew just how sick Mother was and he was capable of observing the treatment in the nursing home. I feel he heard my prayer and answered by urging me to bring her home."

Steve sat quietly and smiled, his eyes surveying mine.

"You and I view God very differently," I said. The practitioner modestly nodded in agreement.

From that moment on we remained cordial to each other, but his beliefs and my growing faith in God caused confusion and many questions.

With Mother's increasing debility and her reluctance to change, hardening lines of resistance formed around her eyes. As I watched her I was stabbed with memories of illnesses never healed in my own body, and of inner wounds that had refused to heal.

As a teenager I had developed an abscessed tooth. Despite earnest prayers, the stubborn infection persisted. However, Mother continued to believe that I would be healed. Not until years later did I have enough courage to have the tooth extracted. A simple procedure that took a moment in a surgeon's office could have ended a problem that caused me years of pain and disgrace. To this day I have a scar.

Unfortunately, the poison had spread to other areas of my body. One night I suffered gruesome humiliation as I watched a bursting abscess. For the first time I saw Mother alarmed. The next day she rushed me to a doctor, who, fearing cancer, lost no time in getting me to a specialist for a biopsy. Fortunately, the test proved benign. God must have been watching over me even then.

My "healings" were not only absolute failures, they were poignant misfortunes that would leave indelible impressions on me for the rest of my life. Yet these episodes, and many others, never caused Mother to falter or question her beliefs.

Talking to Mother about my conversion to Christianity was fruitless. I longed for her to trust Christ in the way that the Bible taught. She thwarted simplistic biblical teachings, preferring the interpretations written by her leader, Mary Baker Eddy.

I was afraid Mother's time was running out. I saw her drowning in a pool of defeat and I wanted her to find the peace and the new understanding of God that I was finding.

Lorraine, a woman who had responded to an ad I'd placed in a local paper, began caring for Mother shortly after we brought her home. She was in her mid-forties, married, and the mother of four children. She had a strong Christian upbringing and her brother was a pastor. She frequently prayed that God would give her an opportunity to talk to Mother about her faith. She wanted to believe that Mother would come to know the Lord as her personal Savior.

One day Lorraine suggested that I go to a Christian bookstore. I'd never heard of a "Christian" bookstore.

When I went I found it full of things to help people know more about God. The store housed an abundant supply of books, magazines, and records. I was overwhelmed by it all. I wanted to purchase everything I could get my hands on.

For weeks I read books about Mother's religion that left me confused and angry. They were shocking exposés of Mother's chosen way of life.

I had often wondered which book had more authority in the minds of Christian Scientists. Mother constantly used Mary Baker Eddy's book, *Science and Health with Key to the Scriptures*. More often than not, I noticed that when she wanted to make a point she referred to it rather than to the Bible.

I began to see warnings in the Bible concerning false teaching. They were frightening messages. I also read about the power of sin in our lives. So much of what I was reading contradicted what I'd been taught for so many years.

> Beloved, believe not every spirit, but try the spirits whether they are of God: because many false prophets are gone out into the world.
>
> Hereby know ye the Spirit of God: Every spirit that confesseth that Jesus Christ is come in the flesh is of God:
>
> And every spirit that confesseth not that Jesus Christ is come in the flesh is not of God: and this is that spirit of antichrist, whereof ye have heard that it should come; and even now already is it in the world.
>
> Ye are of God, little children, and have overcome them: because greater is he that is in you, than he that is in the world. . . .
>
> We are of God: he that knoweth God heareth us; he that is not of God heareth not us. Hereby know we the spirit of truth, and the spirit of error (1 John 4:1-4, 6).

Christian Science denied the reality of matter with these words penned by Mrs. Eddy in *Science and Health* . . . : "Man is not matter; he is not made up of brain, blood, bones, and other material elements."

Flesh is composed of matter, yet Mrs. Eddy taught the nonexistence of it. How then could she explain the reality of Jesus as shown in John 1:1, 14: "In the beginning was the Word, and the Word was with God, and the Word was God. . . . And the Word was made flesh, and dwelt among us . . ."?

In this text the "Word" is Jesus, made flesh and dwelling among us. The Apostle John wrote that anyone who denied that Jesus Christ had come in the flesh was considered to be antichrist.

For weeks I fought the desire to share this unsettling news with Mother. I held back because I thought she wouldn't listen to me. However, after continuously reading these warnings, I knew it would be wrong to keep this information to myself.

My heart was pounding the day I approached Mother. It was extremely important that I be very tactful and sensitive, because her hold on her beliefs was as strong as ever.

Peeking into her room, I observed her pathetic posture. Weakened from the past five years of what seemed like an endless battle, her body occupied an attitude of defeat and I beheld a very frail human being.

When I entered she looked up.

"Mother, how are you?" I asked.

I handed her the pad and she wrote, "I'm in pain."

"What would you like me to do?" I questioned.

She wrote, "Call the practitioner."

After what I'd been reading, a huge knot formed in my stomach, but I respectfully replied, "OK, I'll give him a call; but before I do, may I talk to you about something?"

She nodded her head in agreement, always eager to listen whenever I came into her room.

"I've been reading some material that I purchased in a Christian bookstore and I was hoping that you'd let me share some of it with you," I said softly.

She gave me a skeptical glance but agreed to listen.

"Before I start, I want you to know that what I am going to read might not please you. However, I've found it informative in light of the way you taught me to believe. I won't insist that you listen. If you find it a violation of your privacy, I will respect your wishes and stop reading."

She nodded and I began. Strangely, Mother listened until I'd finished. Her head was thoughtfully resting on the cushioned table in front of her.

"Mother, I know that what I've read is hard for you. I'm not asking you to believe everything. All I ask is that you think about it as an alternative." She gave no visible acknowledgment.

"I'll get Steve now," I said, kissed her cheek softly, and slowly walked from her room.

I continued to be singed by the disconcerting words on the pages of the books I read. I began to pray that God would soften Mother's heart to trust him and him alone.

On three separate occasions we resumed our conversation, giving me more opportunities to share the contents of the literature with Mother. Between these discussions, I prayed that God would reveal himself to her.

By this time, Mother's illness had advanced into the sixth year. For almost three of those years she had been immobile, and her system of recovery had failed. I knew what God was capable of doing in my life, and I prayed to be able to share it with Mother.

I was careful to be neither demanding nor insistent. My purpose was to enable my mother to see that there was another way, and I truly believed that she did a great deal of silent questioning. When she would weep and groan openly because of her unending pain, I felt she couldn't help but consider some of the accounts that I shared with her.

Slowly, but certainly, I started to notice a gradual change. New communication opened up between us, and I saw a ray of hope. For the first time ever, I freely discussed some of my past hurts and we asked each other for forgiveness.

Though Mother still depended on her practitioner, she seemed somewhat complacent and was more lenient toward those of us who didn't think the way she did.

There were painful days entangled with tears and fatigue, but those days were filled with prayer that God would soon free Mother. On days when I found my endurance at its lowest level I often sang along with the words of an album by Jamie Owens I'd been given, titled "Growing Pains." I'd almost worn it out, playing it over and over again. During discouraging times I found myself instantly lifted by the lyrics of one song in particular, "I've Never Had to Go This Far Before."

> *I've done all I know,*
> *Gone as far as I can go,*
> *And I'm prayin' that You will take me*
>   *through.*
>
> *My strength's all run out*
> *And I'm almost starting to doubt*
> *That I can make it;*
> *Oh, Lord, it's up to You.*
>
> *Chorus:*
> *'Cause I've never had to go this far before,*
> *And I don't know if I can do it.*
> *No, I've never had to go this far before,*
> *And I'm countin' on You to see me*
>   *through it.*

My dreams all lie dead,
Can't see any light ahead,
But I'm trustin' You'll carry me along.
'Cause I've heard Your voice,
And my heart has made its choice
To believe You
When You say it won't be long.

Three weeks stretched into months. In October I released the night nurse. I no longer slept in the den, but rarely had a full night's sleep because Mother was always on my mind. Usually I awoke around 3 A.M. to turn her over. It was important, to avoid bedsores, that she not remain in one position for too long.

I was continuing to learn much about caring for an invalid. At the same time I was also learning about God by reading my new Bible. I discovered that he doesn't deal in generalities, but in specifics. I surely had definite needs, not only for myself, but for the immediate care of Mother.

Occasionally, heavy waves of depression would sweep over me. The longer Mother was with us, the more demanding her life became on mine. I experienced times of extreme exhaustion.

Having learned for so many years to "ignore," I was now being taught to "endure." Soon I was memorizing the words to another

song by Owens entitled "Hard Times." I sang
along as the music blared through the house.
It became medicine to my ears:

> *Is the rain fallin' from the sky*
> *Keepin' you from singin'?*
> *Is that tear fallin' from your eye*
> *'Cause the wind is stingin'?*
>
> *Chorus:*
> *Well, don't you fret now, child,*
> *Don't you worry;*
> *The rain's to help you grow,*
> *So don't try to hurry the storm along;*
> *The hard times make you strong.*
>
> *Don't you know a seed could never grow*
> *If there were never showers?*
> *And though the rain might bring a*
>   *little pain,*
> *Just look at all the flowers!*
>
> *I know how long the day can seem*
> *When storm clouds hide His face;*
> *And if the rain dissolves your dream,*
> *Just remember His amazin' grace.*
>
> *Don't you know the sun is always there*
> *Even when the rains fall?*
> *And don't you know the Son will*
>   *always care*
> *When He hears your voice call?*

Mother's pain continued to be her most common complaint and several times I did something I never thought I would do. I called Mother's cousin, the doctor, and asked him to prescribe some medication that I could mix into her food. I felt deceptive and dishonest the few times I did this, but I wanted her pain relieved. I attempted to conceal it, but I knew she suspected something when she began refusing to eat. Some time later I admitted my guilt to Mother and we discussed it. I was amazed at how well she understood.

Christmas was upon us. Mother was still struggling to survive. Despite the turmoil, God blessed me with many unforgettable examples of love from others.

We were asked to put our house on the local "Christmas Tour." To us it was a comfortable and charming home and this was a compliment. Christmas was my favorite time of year and I loved to decorate. Because I was now a Christian, this Christmas would be very special.

The night before the house tour, my sister arrived to help me prepare. She was even more creative than I and with the two of us working together, I knew the house would be beautiful.

Sandy told me that she wanted to give me an early Christmas present and handed me a tiny package. I carefully unwrapped it and found a beautiful handmade ceramic baby Jesus. For years I'd wanted her to make it for me because she had made a crèche for herself that I'd always loved. I was touched deeply by the gift, so much so that I cried. For the first time in my life I knew who Jesus really was and there could never have been a more perfect time for her to have given this present. I was surprised and even more moved when later that evening Sandy presented me with the rest of the crèche. She had hand-painted every piece in beautiful muted shades. I was thrilled.

Between taking care of Mother's needs and the normal requirements of the children and Ted, Sandy and I busied ourselves with the decorating until after three in the morning. When we finished, the house looked like it should have been in a magazine and the fragrance of fresh pine and real fruit and candles filled the air. That night we fell into our beds exhausted, but content.

The next evening hundreds of people walked through our home and admired the creativity displayed everywhere.

Toni and Don were having an informal evangelistic coffee that same night. My desire to see my entire family come to know Christ was intense, so I urged Sandy to go with me. She seemed to enjoy the evening, listening as a young couple told how they used to be, how they had become Christians, and how Christ had changed their lives. I was hopeful that Sandy would see a need for Christ in her life when the time came for a decision. She said she'd liked the evening, but indicated nothing more. However, that night she informed me that her husband, Lee, had been a Christian since he'd been in college. I was surprised that he'd never told me.

Christmas Day was a momentous occasion. Our entire family joined us at our home, and Mother sat in the den, surrounded by those she loved.

For me, becoming a Christian made all the difference in the world. I now understood the true meaning of Christmas. It was a joy for me to say grace before our Christmas dinner; every word was from my heart. Until now, prayers before meals had been a rarity in our home. Lots of things were changing!

As the day came to an end, I realized that Mother had been with us for six months now. In the beginning we had gone full steam ahead. Every day was an exciting adventure. But as time wore on, the complexities of a spiritual battle tugged at me.

The months were filled with intense highs and lows, multitudes of changes for our family, and lots of determination. Using a mixture of courage, despair, and a sense of humor, we managed to get through that period of time more easily than we ever imagined. Our tremulous faith that God was somehow in charge gave us the glimmer of hope that was needed.

6

A New Beginning

Therefore if any man be in Christ, he is a new creature: old things are passed away; behold, all things are become new (2 Corinthians 5:17).

As I hurried through the dishes one night early in January, I mindlessly flipped the radio dial through the stations. I jostled the plates to their proper place in the cabinets, then my attention was drawn to the polished and serene voice of a man on the radio. The background music was a familiar hymn, one I remembered my grandmother playing on the piano. I listened, and soon discovered that I had found a Christian radio station called "Family Radio." This particular program was entitled "Unshackled."

Only moments into the story I knew it was something that Mother should hear. I pulled the plug and rushed into her room, dragging the cord behind me.

"Mother," I said excitedly, "this is the first time I've heard this program, and I thought you'd want to listen to it with me."

Without looking for a response, I plugged the radio in and turned it on. I sat with her as we heard the devastating story of a young fellow who had been on drugs and alcohol. He shared how his selfishness had crushed the lives of those he loved, until eventually his own life was in ruin. However, before it was too late, someone led him to Christ and his life was revolutionized. There were parts of this man's story that both Mother and I could relate to.

"That was some story, wasn't it, Mother?" I asked.

She looked toward me as though a veil had been drawn over her face. She stared at me with a blank, vacant look, drained of even an ounce of emotion. Her silence made me feel uneasy. Then she nodded for the paper and pen.

"Take the radio out!" she wrote.

Feeling as though someone had stabbed me, I removed it, walking away emotionally depleted.

Again those comforting and encouraging words sang through my mind and I found myself rejuvenated: "I've done all I know, gone as far as I can go, and I'm prayin' that You will take me through. My strength's all run out and I'm almost starting to doubt that I can make it; Oh, Lord, it's up to You. . . ."

A few nights later, though the rest of the family was asleep, I was still up trying to finish the laundry. It had been one of those days, and I wondered if I'd ever get caught up. As I sat in the den, watching the eleven o'clock news on TV and folding the clothes, I felt an unexpected urge to peek in on Mother.

When I looked in, I noticed her lying in bed gazing into space. My concern for her grew stronger than ever. The tired weight of uncertainty about the future of her fractured life never seemed to leave her. She was physically wasting away. After years of endless disappointment, waiting for a healing, it appeared that her self-confidence was beginning to erode. She had every reason in the world to be discouraged.

Mother's ability to eat normal amounts of food was hampered because she choked on each morsel. We pureed everything she ate, but each mouthful was an effort for her just to swallow. It was obvious that the muscles of her throat had been affected by this ravaging disease.

"Would you like me to turn you?" I asked.

She nodded, and I began a routine that I could now do with my eyes closed. Bending my knees and leaning toward her, I placed my hands under her shoulder and legs. Cradling her in my arms, I swiftly turned her to the other side. I lifted her head, pulled the pillow from under her, and fluffed it. I replaced her head onto the downy surface, and smoothed back her crumpled, pinched ear. I refitted the sheets around her delicate body, then kissed her gently on the cheek.

"I love you, Mother," I said. She blinked her eyes and smiled faintly. When I walked out of the room my body felt laden with a tender sorrow.

Suddenly I was struck with an idea. Maybe if I shared the "Four Spiritual Laws" with Mother, she would respond and God would change her life, as he had mine.

I whispered a silent prayer, asking God to give me the confidence that I needed to approach her. Moments later I was frantically searching through my desk for a copy of the "Four Laws." I breathed a sigh of relief when I finally located it. Now, did I have the courage to approach her?

Within seconds I was sitting on the floor next to Mother's bed, my heart racing a mile a minute.

"Mother," I began, looking up at her. "I'm really concerned about you. I know you are discouraged about not being healed. That discouragement is only natural. I would like nothing more than to see you completely well.

"I want you back, just the way you used to be. The fact that you're not better doesn't mean you won't be, but it does mean we have to deal with circumstances as they are right now.

"You practice the power of positive thinking over the evidence of matter. Many times you have said that matter isn't real, and yet every day you write notes saying that you are in pain. None of this makes any sense and I believe if you thought about it long enough, you'd feel the same way.

"Mother, your pain is very real and I want you to try to deal with that. I believe something can be done about it, if you would let me order you some medicine. We won't tell anyone; it will be just between you and me."

Mother lay quietly listening as I spoke.

"I've learned so many things since I've become a Christian. I feel freed from the way I used to think. Before, I felt plagued by thoughts that sent me into depression. It's funny, but God has lifted the darkness that clouded my thinking and my mind is so much clearer.

"I'm no longer tormented by the way I used to think. It didn't happen overnight and I'm sure the joy I feel right now isn't as full as it can become. But a new process has begun and it will probably go on until I die." I looked at her tenderly, wanting her to understand.

"You know, Mother, there was a time when my thinking could have destroyed me. And when I look at you, I see you fighting on a very real mental battleground. The problem is, I believe if you continue to go on this way you'll be ultimately disappointed. I would love to see you peaceful and joyful no matter what you have to go through. But I believe that can happen only if you give your life to Christ."

I wondered if she understood what I was talking about.

"Did you know that the Bible is filled with stories of men and women who were not written about because of their perfection, but because of their sinfulness? They allowed God to work through their lives because they were too weak to do it themselves. This weakness made them dependent on God for strength. Their problems became stepping stones to a deeper understanding of who God is. Their afflictions, whatever they were, didn't destroy them.

"Some people feel that if they expose their problems it's a sign of weakness, a sign that God isn't working in their lives. Your illness is not a black spot, Mother. God can use it as a pivotal point to change you just as he used my depression to turn me around."

Once again feeling the joy of all God had done, I began to share how I'd come to know the Lord as my personal Savior. I knew I was speaking out of my own genuine concern for Mother's future.

"God has helped me so much," I told her. "He listens to my every need. Without him I don't think I would have been able to take care of you for as long as I have."

She listened patiently.

"When I came to know the Lord, I prayed a simple little prayer. You can pray that prayer too, Mother, and I truly believe that if you do, you will know God's presence in your life as much as I do."

Summoning up an extra amount of nerve, I took the "Four Spiritual Laws" in my hand and showed her the little booklet.

"May I read this to you?" I asked.

She nodded, and for the next few minutes I read through the pamphlet. I detected no irritation from Mother as I continued to read until I got to the prayer.

"Mother, I know you don't believe in sin. But the Bible clearly teaches that sin is real and that we must be forgiven for it. By just praying a short prayer, God can forgive you of the sin that is in your life and you can be free from it forever.

"Do you mind if I read the prayer?" I asked, looking into her eyes for an answer. She didn't respond one way or the other, so I took it upon myself to read it.

When I finished, I said, "I prayed that prayer right before you asked me to bring you out of the nursing home. I haven't been the same since. I have totally given my life to Christ and with all my heart I want you to experience the wonderful peace that only he can give.

"Someone once told me that within each one of us is a vacuum, an emptiness that can only be filled by God himself. We can have everything in the world in the form of possessions, we can even have perfect health, but we can never experience complete contentment until we are drawn to Jesus for forgiveness. *He* is the peace that everyone is clamoring for. It's so easy. There's nothing to it. All you have to do is ask Christ to come into your life. Do you want to?"

I saw no hint of interest. God had given me another chance with Mother, and she had refused again.

This time, though, I didn't feel that my strength had all run out. I was encouraged by the opportunity to share with her again. When I left her room that night I hoped and prayed that she would mull those words around in her mind and think about what I'd said.

It was so difficult to watch someone I loved suffer so much physically, holding so firmly to something in her life that wasn't helping. Mother was getting no relief from her pain, and the fact that she wouldn't turn for other help frustrated me; but I knew it was not up to me to change her.

Three days later my optimism found revival. Ted and I had been visiting with neighbors.

While there, I excused myself temporarily to go home to check on Mother.

A soft light glowed in the corner of her room as I peered through the doorway, hoping not to wake her. Her eyes were wide open, and she looked up as she sensed my presence.

Entering the room I said, "How are you doing, Mother?"

She indicated that she wanted to say something. Recently, she had become less and less able to write, and we'd learned a new way to communicate by simply going through the alphabet.

Taking the paper and pen in my hands, I started, "A, b, c . . . j, k, l, m, n, o, p, q, r. . . ."

She groaned.

"R?" I questioned.

She nodded her approval. I was perplexed because usually it was p . . . a . . . i . . . n.

"OK, now, a, b?"

She groaned again.

"B?" I asked.

She shook her head.

"Not b?" I questioned. "Then is it a?"

She nodded.

"R . . . a . . . , right?"

She nodded.

"Next letter," I looked at her, "a, b, c, d?"

She moaned.

"R . . . a . . . d?" Many times I was able to

discover what she needed after writing just a few letters, but this time I was stuck.

"Are you ready? A, b, c . . . h, i?" I continued.

She stopped me and suddenly I had it figured out. Startled, I looked at her. "Do you want me to bring in the radio?" I asked as a smile spread over my face. She blinked her eyes, and a faint grin formed around her pale mouth.

I couldn't believe it. She wanted the radio! She wanted the radio! A bubble of joy flipped my stomach around as I flew from the room to the kitchen. I was so full of excitement I didn't think that anything could get me down to earth again.

"I know you're here, God," I said, grinning and looking up. "I just saw you answer a prayer!"

When I put the radio on the table I was so nervous I couldn't find the socket to plug it in.

"There we go." I hoped the electrifying feeling which caused the fluttering in my stomach didn't show too much. But I could tell by her soft and gentle gaze that she read my heart.

"Now, do you want me to tune in the same station we had on the other night?"

With her positive nod, I turned the dial, searching for the station. "Help me find it, Lord," I prayed. Listening for a moment, I heard soft peaceful music. Then the tender voice of a man said, "Good-night, dear heart." His name was Jon Arthur, and he would visit my mother via the radio every night at this hour for the next few years.

Funny, I thought as I walked back to my neighbor's house through the crunching snow, Mother had always called me "dear heart" when I was a little girl.

Happy thoughts stirred through my mind that night. I knew if Mother would listen to Family Radio, God would use it to prepare her heart. And he did.

The next few weeks I observed no real changes in Mother's spiritual condition. The pain she experienced frightened me, but she stood her ground insisting that her cure was inevitable. I remained silent, but continued to pray that God would soon make himself real in her life.

"Only three weeks," the doctors had advised back in June. It was now seven months since we'd transferred Mother from the nursing home. Sometimes it seemed like yesterday. Other times the days dragged on endlessly. However, the adjustment had been a hundred times better than I'd ever hoped.

January had been a difficult month. Carole had left in November and right afterward I'd hired Josephine, a woman from an agency. Because she was a stranger, I never felt completely comfortable with her. But it was the holiday season and I was desperate, so I tolerated things that I normally wouldn't have.

One day while doing errands I stopped long enough to call home to check on things. Josephine answered the phone.

"Mrs. Jamison," she said breathlessly, "I think you had better come home."

"What's wrong, Josephine?" I asked.

Then she started crying and my heart fell into my stomach. "What's wrong?" I asked, almost screaming into the phone. "Tell me, what is it?" Panic for Mother's safety raced through my body.

"Well, your mother has fired me!" she said emphatically.

"She what?" I said.

"She told me she doesn't want me to come back anymore."

"Now, Josephine, I'll be there in a few minutes and we can discuss it."

During the entire ride home I fumed. Mother's audacity in making such a decision without consulting me made me furious. In fact, I was so angry that I didn't go into Mother's room until Ted got home from work that night.

I rationalized Mother's actions to Josephine and begged her to come back the next day. She reluctantly agreed.

When Ted got home from work, we had a long talk. I expressed my impatience with Mother's decision. I pleaded with him to go in and reason with her.

"There is no way I can take care of her twenty-four hours a day. I just will not do that and with stupid actions like this she will force me into it," I said.

"Let's just go in to talk to her together and listen to her side," he suggested calmly.

Mother was sitting in the chair when we walked in. She looked up but showed no sign of remorse for what she'd done.

"Mother, you really shouldn't have fired Josephine without talking to me first. Your actions have caused all kinds of problems. Whatever made you do such a thing?"

For the next forty-five minutes I wrote her messages and we talked. According to Mother there had been a lot going on behind my back. Mother told me numerous things that Josephine had said and done. What Mother said disturbed me, and if it were true, Josephine would have to go.

The following day I confronted her about Mother's accusations. She denied nothing and promised to change. We gave her another chance, but several weeks later I had to let her go.

Arranging for new help wasn't easy and it was something I didn't look forward to. Still, as difficult as the storm had been with Josephine, the sun shone brightly a few days after she had left. I hired a very qualified person we all grew to love and who remained with us until Mother died. Her name was Phyllis

O'Hare, and because of her experience she was into the routine of Mother's care in no time at all.

For several months our family had been attending the church where Lorraine's brother was pastor. Through his consistent Bible teaching, I was discovering some important things about myself and my private values. Over the years my values had not been of the caliber that I now sought to attain. I was somewhat perplexed as my mind sifted through the mountainous stacks of issues in my personal evaluation, issues that needed altering if I was to enhance my moral integrity.

Setting a strong example for my children became one of my highest goals. During the church messages, Pastor Trump provided a way of escape from some of the pitfalls in our home due to our inconsistent standards. My new commitment was to be tested and retested, which caused some painful altercations within the four walls of our home. However, the pain was only temporary as I slowly watched some marvelous changes occur.

Toward the end of the month, Lorraine told me that her brother, Pastor Trump, was going to be in the area and wondered if he could stop by. I felt an excitement building inside as I went into Mother's room with the news.

"Mother, our pastor would like very much to come by to meet you today. Is that OK?"

She looked at me without a hint of hesitation and gave her approval. Naturally I was delighted.

"You'll like him, and you should feel free to ask him any questions you may have. I'll sit in too so I can write for you."

She agreed, and in a little while we had her sitting in her chair, ready and waiting. An air of expectancy enveloped her, an encouraging sign to me.

As the pastor had promised, he arrived a little after noon. Lorraine led him into Mother's room where I was sitting with her.

Mother smiled somewhat warily while Lorraine made the introductions. Pastor Trump took a seat in front of Mother, and his friendly, mild manner put us all at ease.

For the first few minutes he talked about his family and then about his ministry. Mother was able to hold her head up and I watched her eyes sparkle with interest.

Once she saw the pastor's genuine concern, her heart was turned toward the message that he had come to share with her.

"Bonnie has told me that you read your Bible every day. Isn't it a wonderful book?"

She nodded.

Pastor Trump was relaxed and his composure indicated acceptance of Mother. Few people were able to make such a rapid adjustment when talking to her.

"The Bible has the answers to all the questions of life. Wouldn't you agree with that?"

Mother nodded.

"Mrs. Nottingham, I was raised in a home where the Bible was read every day. I knew many Bible stories and had memorized a fair number of verses. But I found there was a great difference between reading the Bible and letting the Bible read me. As its message began to probe my heart, I began to fear dying. I wondered what would happen to me in this life and the next. I knew I wasn't going to heaven. Then one day the way to eternal life that had been shown to me in the Bible so many times before became clear and real. It was as though I had discovered a whole new meaning to life. Indeed I had! I shall never forget it. I was a senior in high school.

"I wonder if I might ask you a couple of questions? All you have to do is nod yes or no. Would that be all right?"

Mother seemed eager for the questions.

"After spending so many years studying your Bible and reading various other writings, do you know for certain, beyond a shadow of a doubt, that you have eternal life and will spend that life in heaven?"

She shook her head no.

"You're probably thinking that it's impossible to know for sure. Most people think that it's a process. You die first and then you know, right?"

She nodded.

"Mrs. Nottingham, did you realize one of the major reasons the Bible was written in the first place was so that by reading it you could know for sure?"

Again Mother indicated a negative response.

"Let's just suppose that God came into this room to speak directly to you and he stood with us and asked you, 'Mrs. Nottingham, why should I let you into my heaven?' Would you say because you read your Bible every day and went to church all the time until you got sick? That you were a very fine person who did commendable things for people? Also that you were a good daughter and wife and mother, that you were a good neighbor, and maybe you tried to keep the Ten Commandments? Would you say that your good deeds outweighed your bad?"

She nodded.

"It's interesting that you should feel that way, because that's the way most people believe that they will enter heaven. But, strangely enough, the Bible doesn't teach that. Getting into heaven has never depended on how good we are. The Bible clearly states that it's a free gift."

With that Pastor Trump flipped through his
Bible and read, "'For by grace are ye saved
through faith; and that not of yourselves: it is
the gift of God: Not of works, lest any man
should boast' (Ephesians 2:8, 9). The Bible
also teaches that the gift of God is eternal life,
a gift that we can have only when we accept
Jesus Christ as our Lord and Savior, for he is
the gift."

Mother looked a little puzzled, but continued listening with her attention focused
squarely on the pastor.

"What I'd like to share with you today is
what God has to say about you and me and
the fact that we don't have to wait until we die
to know if we're going to go to heaven. Does
that sound good to you?"

She nodded with a smile.

"What is a gift? Suppose I were to hand you
a beautifully wrapped package. But before you
took it from my hands, I explained that you
could have it only if you were to come over to
my office and do my typing for a week. Would
that be a gift?"

Mother shook her head no. A slight giggle
came from her throat.

"Of course not; a gift isn't something we
work for. Nor is it something we necessarily
deserve. God tells us in the Bible that heaven
is a free gift—we can't earn it, nor do we deserve it."

The pastor turned the pages of his Bible and said, "This is the reason why God says we don't deserve this gift: 'For all have sinned, and come short of the glory of God' (Romans 3:23); and in the Old Testament God says these words, 'For there is not a just man upon earth, that doeth good, and sinneth not' (Ecclesiastes 7:20). Did you know these words were in the Bible?"

I truly wondered what must have been going through Mother's mind right at that moment. For the past twenty years she'd believed that there was no sin. She had herself convinced that we were all perfect, just like Jesus, and now she was seeing that the Bible doesn't teach that at all. She listened as though she had never heard any of this before.

"Mrs. Nottingham, when God says the words 'all' and 'not one' that is precisely what he means. He means not me, nor you, nor anyone we love. He means not pastors, nor priests, nor people in high places. While God hates sin, he loves us and shows us this love by offering us a free gift. This leaves us in somewhat of a quandary, doesn't it?"

Mother agreed, and Pastor Trump continued thoughtfully.

"A man once went to Jesus and asked him what he should do to be assured of heaven. In other words, what he had to do to be saved from hell. Jesus answered by saying, 'Be ye therefore perfect, even as your Father which is in heaven is perfect' (Matthew 5:48).

"I had a professor in college who asked and answered the question, 'How good do you have to be to get into heaven? As good as God.' I don't think there is anyone as good as God because sin is a part of our nature.

"Some people think that if they do enough good things throughout their lives they sort of cancel out the bad things. We've never done any horrendous, newsworthy sins, so what's the big deal? But God is pure, holy, just, and perfect—and his heaven is the same way. We cannot get into heaven carrying the sin in our lives along with us.

"Looking at it from our standpoint, jealousy, anger, sharp words, just doing our own thing no matter what the cost to another person— these things don't seem to be sin. We'd rather refer to them as mistakes. But in the eyes of God, sin is sin. He despises it no matter how big or small. Because God is perfect, he cannot allow a sinner to come into heaven without having the sin removed.

"When you consider these things, I'm sure you will agree that even the very finest people sin several times a day. That's well over a thousand times a year; and, if we were to live to age seventy, that's more than 70,000 sins. Did you ever wonder what happens to those sins? Since sin would infect God's pure heaven, he, in his merciful love, provided a way by which our sins could be completely removed. This is the wonderful story of his love.

"John 3:16 tells us, 'For God so loved the world, that he gave his only begotten Son, that whosoever believeth in him should not perish, but have everlasting life.' When his Son, Jesus, came to earth, he lived a perfect life. He was the greatest teacher; he healed the sick, gave sight to the blind, cast out demons, and raised the dead. But his greatest work was dying on the cross. You see, while he was on that cross, his blood was being shed to pay the full penalty for all our sin. Now a sinner can be accepted into God's heaven because of what Jesus did." The pastor smiled at Mother as she listened.

"Mrs. Nottingham, isn't it wonderful to know that you and I don't have to pay for our sin? Let me tell you a little story that means a lot to me.

"Many years ago, Nicholas the First, a Russian czar, had the habit of disguising himself as a lower officer. Unknown to him, one of his favorites, a soldier to whom he had given the responsibility of paying the other soldiers, had begun to gamble. Little by little, the soldier gambled away his own money, then he slowly pilfered the funds entrusted to him.

"One day he received word that in the next twenty-four hours his records would be examined and the money counted. Having no idea how much he had absconded, he feared the horrible exposure. He read the records and counted the meager amount of money left. Jotting the amount down on paper, he figured out what he had taken. The total was startling. As he sat staring at the numbers, he wrote these words directly under the figures: 'A great debt; who can pay?'

"Knowing there was no way he could ever repay the debt, he decided that at midnight he would shoot himself. As he sat reflecting upon his failure he began to feel drowsy and, in spite of the trauma he was under, he fell asleep.

"That night Czar Nicholas walked into this young man's fortress. Attracted to the light coming from underneath his door, he opened the door and looked inside. Quietly he walked in, and, looking over the young man's shoulders, he read the paper and everything became clear. It was obvious to the czar that the soldier had been stealing for months.

"Immediately he wanted to arrest him. However, suddenly he felt a generous impulse as his eyes fell on the words, 'A great debt; who can pay?' Moved by compassion, he wrote one word under that line and slipped quietly out of the room.

"Suddenly the young man awoke and realized that it was long past midnight. He picked up his gun and placed it to his forehead. As he was about to pull the trigger, his eyes caught the word 'Nicholas' on the sheet of paper. He knew it had not been there when he went to sleep. Unbelieving, he dropped his gun and checked the signature with other documents to see if it was authentic. It was genuine. Knowing the czar had been there and discovered his guilt, yet had paid the debt for him, overwhelmed him.

"The following morning, a messenger from the royal palace brought the exact amount of the missing money. When the inspector arrived to examine the safe and the records, everything was in order. Nicholas had paid the debt in full.

"This is a human illustration of what Jesus has done for us. The word *Nicholas* spoke peace to that officer's heart. The name that speaks peace to me is *Jesus*. Because of him and his work on the cross, all my sins have been cleared. This same absolution is for you, because God '. . . hath made him to be sin for us, who knew no sin; that we might be made the righteousness of God in him' (2 Corinthians 5:21).

"When one decides to receive Christ as his Savior, he must invite him into his heart through prayer, which is simply talking to God. It is good for this person to form in words his heart's desire. Such a prayer might express thanks to God for his love and for sending his Son, Jesus Christ, to die on the cross for our sins. It would ask for mercy, for forgiveness of sins. Through this prayer a person can open his heart to God and by faith receive Christ as his personal Savior.

"Mrs. Nottingham, is that a prayer that you could honestly pray to God?"

Knowing that Mother was coming face to face with the greatest spiritual decision of her life, our hearts held a moment of tension. Relief came when she nodded her head in the affirmative.

"Would you be willing to pray quietly in your heart while I pray for you out loud?"

The moment we had all been praying for for so many months had finally arrived and joy filled the room with a quiet expectancy. We bowed our heads as the pastor prayed quietly and lovingly.

When he finished, Mother looked up. Her face radiated a glorious countenance and a broad smile swept across her face. Her eyes softened to a warm blue, glistening as tears rolled down her cheeks. Though she was unable to speak, her vocal cords gave a sound of rejoicing.

Mother's spiritual sensitivity had remained strong enough so that at this moment she believed the truth.

Finally, because of her decision, the worst was over. Her efforts to deal unrealistically with pain would come to a close. Today marked the start of a fresh focus on what life was all about, as well as a period of restoration. Whatever lay ahead, God would renew our strength and give us the inexhaustible courage we would need to go from here. Surely he'd provided a new beginning.

As immeasurable peace filled my heart, I knew this moment would leave a vivid mark on the rest of my life.

It was January 26, 1978.

7

She Needed the Quiet

*So we do not lose heart. Though our
outer nature is wasting away, our
inner nature is being renewed every
day (2 Corinthians 4:16, RSV).*

The familiar anxieties over Mother's eternal destiny had finally been put to rest. She had at last made peace with God. Day by day a relaxed communication grew between us as I observed the reality of God in her life.

Her frail, weak body showed no signs of renewed strength. I suspected that since she now had a personal relationship with God, he would relieve her suffering quickly. Besides, I couldn't bear to see her in such agony much longer.

Things began to happen in rapid succession, some very good, others not so good. Before I knew it she asked to have her practitioner relieved from his duties. My sister had been visiting during the time Mother made this decision and Sandy made the final call. We were encouraged by this act and agreed to eliminate the use of a practitioner.

But the following week, while I was away, Mother was in such excruciating pain that she insisted Brooke phone the practitioner. When Brooke called, her request for services was flatly refused.

Immediately upon my return home, Mother wanted me to contact a new practitioner. I stood before her in disbelief. Vexation flooded my body and my throat became tight and dry.

"I will *never, ever* call another practitioner again, Mother. I am tired of explaining your symptoms to people who don't even believe in symptoms." My words were sharp and angry. With nothing more to say, I stormed out, slamming the door behind me.

Running to my room, I threw myself across the bed and wept. Mother's indomitable ways still could spread negativism everywhere. That, combined with the shame of my angry reaction, made me feel miserable. I was at my wit's end, and I prayed for God to intervene.

"God," I cried out, "I can't cope with this any longer."

Because Mother's life expectancy was so unpredictable all kinds of alternatives went through my mind, from putting her back into a nursing home to sharing the responsibility with Sandy.

In the quietness of my room I confessed my inability to love Mother the way I should and admitted my anger over the entire situation.

As only God can, he reached down and touched my weary body. I sensed him coaxing me back to Mother's room to ask her to forgive me for the way I'd spoken. It was the first time I realized that I had a responsibility not only to ask God's forgiveness, but to ask it of Mother as well.

Apologizing was something that hadn't been a habit in my life. To admit wrongdoing wasn't easy, but it was a necessary ingredient to sweep away the ugliness. Bitter words cause hurt that can never be forgotten until forgiveness is offered. That day I was to learn the powerful, purifying effects that come from two simple words, "I'm sorry."

It must have been hours before my mind was cleared and I finally pulled myself together enough to return to Mother's room. She was sitting in the chair and looked up when I entered.

I took the seat across from her and gently touched her tiny bony hands.

"I love you, Mother," I said, and with that came a rush of tears and sobbing.

Finally gaining my composure, I said, "Please forgive me for the way I talked to you this morning. I had no right to raise my voice and slam the door like that. I know I must have hurt your feelings. I'm truly sorry. Will you forgive me?"

She nodded and tweaked her eyes to tell me

she loved me. Only a mother forgives so easily!

"What I ask you to forgive is my temper; I was out of control. But I really meant what I said. I can no longer allow a practitioner to visit you here. When you accepted Christ you were sick and spiritually defeated. God wants to change all of that and he will accomplish in you something that you are not able to do through your own strength.

"The Bible teaches that the mind is controlled either by God or by Satan. We have the power to choose whose side we want to be on. In order to know the mind of God, you must trust him implicitly. If you continue to think the way you have I'm afraid you will be ultimately disappointed. God has liberated you and allowed you another choice, as well as another chance."

She smiled in agreement, directing her eyes to the note pad and pen. "Take me to the hospital," were the words written when I finished going through the alphabet.

Surprised and mystified, I fumbled for words.

"You want me to take you to the hospital?" I asked. "Are you sure?"

It seemed that this was precisely what she desired, and I was baffled.

By Monday morning, February 20, 1978, all arrangements had been made and an ambulance pulled up to our house and whisked her off to a doctor's office, a prerequisite for hospital admission. Following behind in my car, I prayed for calm. I had been extremely nervous prior to leaving the house.

A neurologist gave Mother a thorough examination, after which he called me in privately and asked me routine questions including what I thought she might have.

"I've been doing my homework," I said proudly, "and my unprofessional opinion is that Mother has Amyotrophic Lateral Sclerosis." This disease is commonly known as ALS or Lou Gehrig's disease.

"Smart girl," he said with a grin. "And I concur. The only curious thing I can find is that this started with swallowing difficulty and normally ALS begins at the feet and works its way up. It's surprising that she has lived as long as she has. Ordinarily, when ALS begins in the throat the patient dies before it ever advances through the body because, once it reaches the lungs, pneumonia sets in. A simple cold spreads like a raging fire.

"I would like to admit her into the hospital and do a series of tests. The entire procedure will take approximately a week. Unfortunately, the tragic delay has left few options."

I agreed with his decision, and we returned to the examining room, where Mother was waiting. The doctor smiled at her.

"I understand you were an RN?" he questioned warmly. I had informed him of this during the course of our conversation in his office.

Mother flashed him a broad smile, and he proceeded to test her reflexes.

"Interesting. Typical ALS." He nodded toward me.

Then he checked her heart, her mouth, and asked her to stick out her tongue. She couldn't.

When the doctor asked her if she wanted to go into the hospital she shook her head. However, when I reminded her that it had been her idea in the first place, she nodded toward the doctor.

While walking back to his office, I noticed a puzzled look on his face.

"What's the matter?" I questioned.

"I'm not sure. Some things about her examination definitely point to ALS, but others don't. She appears to be able to do more than she lets on." The fact that her speech went first and that her arms were rigid, instead of limp like her legs, troubled him.

"Has anything traumatic happened to her?"

I explained about the automobile accident.

He suggested that there was a slight chance that Mother's illness was psychosomatic. I was shocked! Then he repeated a story about a man who didn't do anything for ten years and then suddenly began to walk.

"What do you want done?" he questioned.

"I'd like Mother admitted into the hospital.

I have to know what we're dealing with once and for all. Last summer her prognosis was only three weeks. I must plan for the future."

"OK, then, we'll get things underway immediately."

Mother was taken by ambulance from the doctor's office to the hospital across the street where she was placed in a waiting area until the admittance procedures were completed.

Despite the new environment, she appeared quiet and remarkably calm. It was a special time for us. I had remembered to bring my Bible and "Our Daily Bread," a devotional booklet that I had grown to love. I read every psalm that I could find on the comfort of God and discovered that the words had an amazingly positive effect on both of us.

Within an hour Mother was settled. Activity filled her room as the nurses and doctors became acquainted with her. Assuming an assertive posture, I quickly informed them of Mother's likes and dislikes, trying to foster my expectations upon them. I hoped for a workable balance among all of us, but I soon discovered that they were far too busy to learn what had taken me months to understand.

The nurses had given me the freedom to stay as late as I wanted, assuring me that my presence was welcome and necessary. I was relieved when Mother was willing to take medication for the first time. Before I left that night she was relaxed.

The day had been emotionally grueling for both of us. Wrenched by fatigue I headed for home, thoughts swirling in my mind concerning Mother's future. I felt a sinking sense of loss as I thought about her shattered life.

It was late by the time I arrived, but Ted had waited up for me and listened thoughtfully as I revealed the day's events. His interest comforted me. Yet I wondered . . . am I being a good wife and mother? Am I cheating my family of precious time? Too tired to let my doubts generate anxiety, I quietly gave them to the Lord and fell asleep.

My heart skipped a few extra beats with hope as I drove back to the hospital the following morning. I couldn't erase the word "psychosomatic" from my mind. I almost wished it were true. Maybe God had a miracle planned. Wouldn't it be something if she were healed? My joy was hard to contain.

But one look at Mother and my bubble completely burst. She looked dreadful, worse than I had ever seen her. Hoping she hadn't noticed me, I turned and walked out to the hallway. I stalled for time to gain my composure and to hide my tears. When I finally entered the room, I couldn't think of a thing to say to cheer her.

The ordeal with this blunt and cruel disease

had taken its toll, and yet I wasn't sure I could let her go. She had been such a special part of my life. I wanted Mother to live, no matter what her condition.

The following morning, when I went to her room, the bed was stripped. A sickening feeling fell to the pit of my stomach. *She's dead,* I thought. *I know she's dead.*

I hurried out the doorway and there to my left, my eyes caught Mother sitting in a geri-chair, all slumped over to one side and unable to pull herself up. My heart raced as I rushed over to straighten her, provoked that she'd been permitted to remain in such an uncomfortable position.

The week was filled with endless hours at the hospital, talking to the doctors and assisting the nurses with Mother's care. Yet, keeping busy was therapy for me.

Every spare moment I spent with Mother we talked about God and his provisions to those who love him. I watched her trust in him grow stronger even though her body grew weaker.

Together we prayed through Psalm 25:

> To you, O Lord, we pray. Don't fail us, Lord, for we are trusting you . . . none who have faith in you will ever be disgraced for trusting . . . show us the path where we should go, O Lord, point out

the right road for us to walk. Lead us;
teach us; for you are the God who gives
us salvation. We have no hope except in
you . . . look at us instead through eyes
of mercy and forgiveness, through eyes of
everlasting love and kindness. You are
good and glad to teach the proper path
to all who go astray; we know you will
teach us the ways that are right and best
if we humbly turn to you; and when we
obey you, every path you guide us on is
fragrant with lovingkindness and truth
. . . friendship with God is reserved for
those who reverence you . . . with us you
share the secret promises. Our eyes are
ever looking to you for help, for you alone
can rescue us. Come, Lord, and show us
your mercy, for we are helpless, overwhelmed, in deep distress; our problems
go from bad to worse. Oh, save us from
them all! See our sorrows; feel our pain;
forgive our sins; Oh, let it never be said
that we trusted in vain! (my own para-
phrase)

One day while I was getting Mother out of
bed, I became aware that she was staring at
herself in a large mirror that stood directly
across from us. This was the first time she had
seen herself in a couple of years. I knew her
image was not what she'd remembered, and I

was certain it was one that she soon wanted to forget, for she quickly turned her head away. I wondered what she must have thought during that split second. Did she recognize herself? Now a mere ninety-five pounds, she was a fraction of her normal weight. Aching for her, I wished I could wipe the picture from her mind.

Each day she became more weary. Not knowing what the next day would bring, I called Sandy to come for a visit. She stayed two days, during which time we discussed funeral arrangements and purchased a burial outfit.

On Wednesday morning Mother underwent an electromyography (EMG). During the painful test the doctors had to inject eight pins into the muscles of one arm and one leg. If there was damage or disease in the nerves or muscles it would show in the results, indicating the seriousness of her condition. She also went through a series of blood tests.

My greatest fears were confirmed, and a sense of helplessness crept through me as I heard the doctor's report. The test results clearly indicated that Mother was a victim of ALS, an incurable and debilitating neurological disease. Along with this, she had severe and painful arthritis and pericarditis, an inflammation surrounding the lining of her heart. If the prognosis was accurate, Mother would not live past "six months, at best." Since her brain would never be affected, she would be clearly aware of each day until her death.

Ted and I had some serious thinking and planning to do in a hurry. We had been informed that Mother would be released from the hospital in a few days. In order for us to have a break from the tensions surrounding this situation, as well as time to do some personal reevaluation, arrangements had been made to put Mother into a very nice nursing facility.

Two weeks later, without a moment's hesitation, Ted made the final decision to bring Mother back home to live with us. He had watched the efficiency of everyone over the past seven months. He'd even become personally involved in her physical care by helping us lift her when he was home. I was sure he'd grown to love her deeply. Now, very confidently, he had arrived at a decision. How different it was from the first time! And how I needed the strength of his conviction because I was doubtful that we could continue to handle Mother indefinitely.

We knew, no matter what, we were unable to control Mother's destiny. We were simply part of a cast of people in her life playing our roles. We determined to be her support team, giving hope to what looked like despair, for as long as it was needed.

Some time before I had read that "To a winner, defeat is a pause between two victories; to a loser, defeat is a way of life." Now in partnership with each other and God, whatever the price, we were out to win. We would not allow defeat to enter the game.

A transformation began. With the strength of God and our growing faith in him, we were going to defy the skeptics. None of us was qualified to fulfill the responsibilities that God had arranged for us. However, with the Apostle Paul we could say, "Therefore I take pleasure in infirmities, in reproaches, in necessities, in persecutions, in distresses for Christ's sake: for when I am weak, then am I strong." (2 Corinthians 12:10). Sometimes it was painful, other times it was sad, but it was never regrettable.

There was a time when I thought that God would heal Mother. I was convinced that that was what he intended to do. Now I feel that God allowed me to have that hope to keep me going at times. Even though the elders of the church prayed over Mother for healing, and friends gathered around her bed to do likewise, she remained trapped in her motionless body. We looked for physical healing. What our eyes could not observe was the transforming beauty of God's inner healing.

Slowly, God began to build bridges of love between himself and us, spanning the rivers of our past, extending into the future of our eternal hope in heaven. We were not going to be unhappy statistics, spreading tales of sorrow to the world around us. Instead, we would tell where we found our source of strength.

In addition to attending a wonderful Bible church, I became actively involved in a weekly ladies' Bible study. All that I learned I shared with Mother. Together, we discovered that God has a purpose for our lives when we become Christians. We move from darkness into light. It's like donning a new pair of eyes.

When Mother's restoration began, her inner turmoil and restlessness were miraculously replaced by the peace of God. Despite the condition and circumstances that threatened to crush her, she had absolute confidence in knowing that she was safe and secure in God's hands. Mother's life became a sequence of events in which God was Master. After he finally got her attention, she gave her all to him.

As the weeks passed swiftly into months and the seasons moved into years, Mother's heartbeat became the heartbeat of all who had grown to love her. The smile that radiated whenever friends walked into her room was carried within them to the world outside.

Denial was washed completely from her thinking; bargaining with God was gone. Both were replaced by a total and complete trust in her Savior. Refusing to be engulfed by the walls of illness, she sought God's answers to each need.

Often I teased her about the fact that as weak as she was, she remained a strong parent. "Once a mother, always a mother," I joked. But it was really true.

When the demands of life got the best of me, her "motherly" role resurfaced. Searching my eyes, she'd have me write her message . . . usually telling me where I could find what God said about being a better wife and mother. She constantly upheld me, and many others, in prayer.

Some days were absolutely tedious. The normal demands at home were complicated at times with a rigorous schedule of outside interests. I'd discovered the privilege and joy of sharing my faith through the ministry of Christian Women's Club and I became an active partner with Toni in our "Joy in the Morning" Bible study, reaching out to the neighborhood women. My energy was sapped, and at times I took my frustration out on the rest of the family. These were shameful occurrences that held severe consequences if left unheeded. We marveled as we watched God alter many negative situations, turning them into positive experiences.

Mother spent a great part of her days reading the Bible. She quickly became more familiar with it than I was, keeping in close touch with the Lord. Her unquenchable desire for God was fascinating.

Praying became her ministry. She prayed that her children and grandchildren would come to know Christ as she did. We prayed together every night that God would move in the lives of everyone that we loved.

One Christmas she gave each of her grandchildren, and my brother, a beautiful Bible. Inside the covers were written these words: "Jesus loves us this we know, for the Bible tells us so. Christmas is the birthday of Jesus. I love Jesus and you too. Love, Nanna" and "Fear thou not; for I am with thee. Be not dismayed; for I am thy God. I will strengthen thee; yea, I will help thee; yea, I will uphold thee with the right hand of my righteousness" (Isaiah 41:10).

The following two years, my sister's four children and Brooke attended Christian camps as a gift from Mother. Brooke had already come to know Christ, but during this time David, Christopher, Jennifer, and Robin asked Christ to be their Savior.

These experiences brought unbelievable joy to Mother. Despite her inability to talk, pride overflowed in the knowledge that God allowed her what few grandparents enjoy: She had provided the vehicle through which her grandchildren had become Christians.

The last three years that Mother lived, the same women helped with her physical needs. Much was required of them. Mother was a very precious gift and we wanted her to have nothing but meticulous care. In the beginning, it was awkward for everyone. Handling Mother wasn't easy, but with time and adjustments, their concern and love for her grew.

Phyllis worked three days a week, Lorraine helped every Wednesday, and Anne Hartman, a dear woman from my Bible study, came every Monday. On occasion, Lorraine's daughter, Donna, pitched in. Toni and Carlee always remained available. Our family took over in the evenings.

Then I hired Betty Moore, who was in charge each Sunday as well as on Saturdays if we had plans. With the exception of Betty, all the other women had families, so in the summers I hired a college nursing major, Phyllis Adams, the daughter of a personal friend.

We felt honored to have each of the women. They were special and unique, exhibiting qualities of generosity, compassion, and love far beyond the call of duty. Their hearts were tender and sensitive toward Mother and her condition. They provided companionship, encouragement, and humor. Sometimes they even interrupted their own personal plans in order to help us.

Whether they ministered the duties of bathing, feeding, giving medication, applying physical therapy, reading to her, praying with her, or just chatting, they provided just what Mother required. Their actions were the medicine Mother needed to help endure some very painful times. Although she was totally bedridden during the last three years, her care was superior. With her income limited, their pay was not what they could have earned elsewhere, but the money didn't seem to be of significance to them.

Our three children, John, Lisa, and Brooke, became a team of their own, contributing immensely to Mother's happiness as well as participating in the myriad of requirements. Their individual personalities blossomed as they learned to give of themselves, expecting absolutely nothing in return. Before long, they were able to do everything for her, often filling in when the "nurses" were unavailable. I always felt confident whenever I left Mother alone with them.

During the evenings, if Ted and I went out, the children took care of her; and if they went to bed before we got home there was always a note waiting for us on the kitchen table. One such note read, "Mom, Nan says she wants *lots* of cake and ice cream. I was going to give it to her, but didn't know if you wanted me to because you weren't here. Good-night." Ice cream and cake before bed had become a nightly ritual.

At first Lisa had difficulty adjusting to the fact that Mother was unable to talk. One afternoon she expressed her concern to me. "Mom," she said, "I've noticed how easy it is for everyone to go into Nan's room and talk to her. Brooke just goes in and talks as though she was having a two-way conversation. I want to be able to do that too and so I've decided that I'm going to feed Nan her ice cream and give the medication every night until I become more at ease." Within a short time, talking to Mother became natural for Lisa and she and Nanna enjoyed many wonderful times together as a loving relationship grew.

Our children felt an exceptional and unique kind of love toward their dying grandmother. It touched Ted and me deeply. We were proud of the way they handled themselves, especially when they had to give up something they'd looked forward to doing in order to help with her.

During one of these times Mother had accidentally wet the bed. Tired, I permitted it to get the best of me and told her angrily that I couldn't handle it. I went to my room crying, carrying with me a heavy weight of ugliness. Ashamed again, I asked God to forgive me. At times it seemed that I was constantly asking for forgiveness. Moments later I regained my composure.

Walking toward her room, I heard laughing and joking. Not believing my ears, I quietly peeked around the corner. There, to my surprise, were John and Lisa lifting Mother onto the commode. When they saw me they motioned for me to stay away. Stepping back, my heart was lifted as I recognized their sensitivity toward Mother and me, as well as their loving willingness to do a job that most people would never touch. I knew when all was said and done, they would feel a deep sense of satisfaction in the way they had handled the problem. God had certainly wrapped our family in a blanket of love as he guided us in the right direction.

Even though we experienced some difficult times, we never permitted ourselves to consider Mother a burden. Burdens are for people who have no answers, who don't know the joy of giving and expecting nothing in return and who are unable to experience the thrill of having a personal and meaningful relationship with another person in the living God.

When we began to see that the circumstances surrounding Mother's illness were not going to change, we decided our attitudes would.

We never glossed over the physical suffering that Mother had to endure each day, nor did we push aside the personal upheaval that went along with the requirements of her daily needs. Mother's care simply grew to be a natural part of our lives. We found that the little things, a visit from a friend, fresh flowers, manicures, a tube of new lipstick or fragrant perfume, a special card or note, lifted her and added a sense of normalcy to her life.

We gave Mother room to question what was happening to her, to cry if she chose, and very often we cried with her. She had room to doubt, to reason, and to work through some extreme emotions. Difficult experiences take time to heal, lots of time.

We were available to listen, even though it was hard for her to share her deep feelings. And we always tried to exercise caution when giving advice.

Romans 22:15 tells us to "rejoice with those who rejoice, and weep with those who weep." This was the kind of love that surrounded Mother.

There had been a time when she isolated herself from people who had a genuine interest in her. When we first brought her home, she wanted to see very few people. We rarely invited friends or neighbors in to visit. Her secretiveness made it hard on those of us who offered to help.

However, her acceptance of Christ was a major turning point and her attitude changed. She made new friends and discovered that people accepted her just the way she was. Her personal worth was not based on her physical health. These friends stood by her and shared her hurts. She learned to accept the hurdles her disease placed in her path and turn them into challenges.

People were the key that God used to open the doors of reality. She learned from them as they touched her life and gave her hope and promise. One such group was the Muscular Dystrophy Association who willingly offered to take care of many of Mother's monthly expenses. They were a tremendous financial support to us and their generosity was gratefully accepted.

Television and Family Radio became helpful companions. Through these channels Mother heard God's Word. She learned that he gave his grace each day. Trusting in that, she refused to be weighted down by looking beyond the moment. God taught us to take one day at a time.

Nevertheless, it hurt to watch her pain and suffering. Often pep talks seemed insincere. But the pain, instead of causing her to drift away, brought Mother closer to God. She viewed him as the God of the Bible. She became a better person and we all became kinder.

Was Mother's suffering unjust? Looking way back to the beginning, my initial response would have been an unequivocal yes. Yet, though initially we suffered from bitterness over this tragic illness, we discovered that Mother's infirmity was not sent by God to punish her. If we allowed him the freedom he wished in this situation, much more good could be achieved than if the affliction had never occurred. It brought about changes that would last a lifetime.

Because of this, my answer has changed. It was not injustice, but a sovereign God at work. God used the only event that he knew would draw us to himself. He taught us hour by hour to trust him as he transformed the disease into a cause for celebration.

This seemingly awful affliction gave birth to a profound, lasting faith, not only in Mother but in our entire family. God could see what we couldn't, the end from the beginning!

8

Cutting the Tie That Binds

. . . and I will dwell in the house of
the Lord for ever (Psalm 23:6b).

When the world that I've been living in
    collapses round my feet
When my life is shattered and torn
Though I'm windswept and battered
I can cling to His cross and
I find peace in the midst of my storm.

There is peace in the midst of my storm-
    tossed life
There's an anchor, there's a rock that I
    can stand upon
Jesus sails my vessel so I'll fear no alarm
He gives me peace in the midst of my
    storm.

When in twenty-four short hours,
    years of living come down to moments

And when life's final picture comes into
view
In the dark room of my suffering
There's a light come shining through
God gives me peace in the midst of the
storm.

When my body has been broken,
It's racked with pain and misery
When the doctors have done their best
yet look forlorn
Jesus comes to make my bedside
A cathedral of hope and love
And brings His peace right into the midst
of my storm.

He gives me peace in the midst of my
storm-tossed life
There's an anchor, there's a rock that I
can stand upon
Jesus sails my vessel so I feel no alarm
He gives me peace in the midst of the
storm.

Peace, peace wonderful peace
He gives me peace in the midst of the
storm.

(Adams/Dimension)

I began to notice Mother slowly declining as
Christmas of 1980 approached. Until that time
her condition had stabilized. In January, she

got her first urinary infection which attacked her frequently from that time on.

The months that followed were filled with adjustments to new medications and moments that seemed long, dark, and bleak. All the Lord required of us was to trust him.

Throughout the four years Mother had lived with us, she caught numerous colds, but they never lasted more than a few days. However, in early April she caught the cold that we dreaded. We knew that her slight sniffle could mean the end of one of the most important chapters in our lives, a chapter that could never be re-written. Mother's body had little resistance now. Nine years had passed since she showed the first signs of the consuming disease, but the end seemed radically shortened.

A switch was thrown in my mind, releasing uncontrollable thoughts. I didn't want to think or guess, but instinctively I knew the end was near.

On April 20, 1981, I stood alone in a crowd of cheering, excited spectators watching the early finishers of the Boston Marathon. Ted finished, breaking his personal record. My feet and body were milling with the crowds on the streets, as I talked with Brooke and some friends, but my mind was in New Jersey. Hit by waves of doubt, I strove to maintain my composure.

Tuesday, April 21, we pulled into our driveway. A worried expression filled Phyllis's eyes when I greeted her. "Your mother is very sick," she said.

I whispered a silent prayer, thanking the Lord for keeping her alive until we arrived home. My greatest worry was that, having taken care of her for four years, I wouldn't be with her at the moment of her death.

Throwing my shoulders back and arming myself with optimism, I walked into Mother's room. She smiled a weak, delicate smile. My heart disappeared into the pit of my stomach as I saw death written all over her. Prompted by the fear of what lay ahead, my muscles stiffened with tension. I forced myself to return the smile. Hugging her, I hung for a moment on her neck, then I hid my worry and grief.

"Phyllis told me you don't feel too well."

She nodded.

"I'll give the doctor a quick call, OK?"

She was ready.

After Phyllis filled me in on the four days we were away, she left and I phoned the doctor. I also called Sandy and tried to reach my brother, Charley, to let them know what was happening.

It was Easter vacation. The children were on spring break, and the "nurses" were off duty for the rest of the week. I had full charge of Mother, day and night.

Wednesday morning, while she was sitting

on the commode, she seemed to lose her breath, gasping for air. I quickly lifted her back into her bed, then raised it a little. As I watched her regain her color, my panic lessened. The doctor was not supposed to come until the following day, but I called him asking him to come sooner. He warmly obliged.

"Mother," I told her as we waited for the doctor, "if you're frightened, I'll call an ambulance and take you to the hospital. I'll stay with you there, I won't leave you!"

She shook her head.

"We have a prayer chain at church. Shall I call and ask them to pray?"

She smiled.

The doctor arrived and gave her a thorough examination. He showed no signs of worry in front of her. But, as we walked out to the kitchen together, I read concern on his face.

"Be honest with me, Doctor. What is it?" I said. We'd always had a comfortable relationship.

"She's very sick, my dear . . . looks like pneumonia. My advice to you would be to keep her here where she is loved and content. She'll never get the kind of treatment in the hospital that she's been receiving here."

"What shall I do now?" I asked.

"Whatever traditions your family has—it won't be long," he said with a sympathetic tone in his voice.

Everything he said sounded so final. As I walked him to the front door, I thanked him and kissed his cheek. He smiled and said, "God bless."

I was glad I didn't have to share Mother with the nurses that week. I had her all to myself. Despite a lack of sleep, I wasn't consumed with confusion, worry, or bewilderment. I felt strong and in control, oddly rejuvenated. Mother's room seemed filled with quiet as our lives were touched with God's comfort, that special peace that passes all understanding.

Mother had eaten very little food for over two weeks. Thursday she ate practically nothing. I called Pastor Trump, who had visited her faithfully over the years. He spent all of Friday morning with her reading verses that pertained to heaven and her assurance of eternity. The words were beautiful and brought comfort to both of us. Mother listened restfully, and when we left her room, I asked the pastor what he thought. He only shook his head and murmured that she didn't look well.

For the first time all week I cried. As I choked back the tears, he said, "You'll really miss her, won't you?"

I nodded as I thought about the loving yet difficult interlude the past four years had provided. It had been a time to trust God, a time of giving up some normal pleasures, and a time when we finally grew out of the self-centered shells we had worn so comfortably for years. We had experienced such joy and peace within our family simply because we were willing to give. *When she dies, I'll never stop missing her,* I thought to myself.

I'd kept very close records of Mother's vital signs as well as her consumption of food and her elimination. She experienced increased difficulty in breathing and I had trouble keeping her comfortable. I constantly turned her from one side to the other and rearranged her arms and legs, hoping to relieve some of the suffering.

Each day brought further complications. She was now unable to control her bladder and bowels some of the time, and she relied heavily on me for encouragement and consolation.

The calm that I felt throughout that week amazed even me. I was grateful, because I knew it helped Mother.

From the beginning of Mother's conversion to Christianity, we had been completely free to discuss the meaning of life and death. We chose to believe God's account and our faith in an afterlife rested squarely upon the truths written in the Bible. This fortified us, keeping us from falling apart during this crucial time.

The quality of our relationship was rich because it was based on mutual love and respect.

There could be no apologies—God was in charge and Mother was insightful enough to know what was happening.

The phone rang often as friends called to see what they could do. Sandy kept in touch daily. By Friday she still couldn't decide what she should do. "Come now," I said. I felt an urgency as I thought about the words I'd uttered. As much as I didn't want to admit it, our days with Mother were coming to an end.

Still unable to reach my brother, I called my Aunt Helen and Uncle Russ to come for the evening. I felt that they would want to spend some time with her since they had remained very close to Mother. They seemed eager to come.

Friday evening was a special night for Mother. Sandy, her husband, Lee, and their four children arrived about the same time as Uncle Russ and Aunt Helen. Everyone enjoyed the evening. Uncle Russ, full of fun as usual, added a light touch to what could otherwise have been a depressing occasion. When my uncle and aunt left, they took Brooke home with them, leaving Ted and me to ourselves. John was away for the weekend and Lisa was at college. It felt odd not having them with us, especially at this time.

Mother was always happy when everyone she loved was around. She rallied and was surprisingly alert when I was preparing her for the night. After giving her the medication, I read the Bible and prayed with her. This was something we had done together every night for three years. Then I turned on Family Radio and kissed her good-night. Her eyes were bright and she blinked them several times to let me know she loved me. Even though we knew how much we loved each other, there was never a day that we didn't say it.

"I love you, too, Mother," I said as I walked from the room, hoping I'd find her in good spirits in the morning.

Saturday morning began on schedule, just like any other day. I awoke before 6 A.M. and went immediately downstairs to check Mother.

She was awake and her eyes were wide open. She seemed eager to get up.

When I lifted her, she felt different to me, much different. For years she had been dead weight. Today she felt like a rag doll. Her body was lifeless and dripping with perspiration.

"You don't feel well, do you, Mother?"

She was too weak to reply.

Foreboding thoughts filtered through my mind as I immediately changed the wet bed-sheets and cleaned Mother, getting her back into bed as quickly as I could. Every thought and action seemed accelerated. Everything I'd considered the day before was approaching reality now. She was dying and I knew it. I wanted desperately to delay it, just for a little while longer. Was it wrong to want God to postpone her death?

Tucking the covers around her body, I kissed her cheek and said, "I'll be right back."

I felt as though I was flying through the house as I ran upstairs and into our room where Ted was getting dressed.

"Ted," I said, almost breathless, "I know you and Uncle Russ have plans to play golf today and I really want you to go, but please," and I hesitated, trying to keep the tears from choking my words, "please, spend a little time with Mother before you go." I couldn't say, "because I think she's going to die today." Those words would have been much too difficult to say.

His eyes held a serious look, but he asked no questions.

"Please wake Sandy," I said as I raced back down the stairs. "I don't want to leave Mother alone for one minute."

One by one the family arrived in her room. I truly wished our children could have been there. I know Mother missed them, but I consoled myself by remembering the many times that they were there when she needed them the most. I knew there wasn't any chance of getting them home in time.

Ted walked out to the kitchen and asked me to join him. "I'm calling Russ to cancel the match. I don't want to play golf today." Grief and confirmation of Mother's imminent death were written all over his face. I hugged him because I was happy that he'd chosen to stay home without any prompting from me.

I went back into Mother's room. She seemed perfectly peaceful and quiet. There appeared to be no fear. She was free to die, leaving no unfinished business. She indicated that she had no pain.

No pain, I thought. God had already started to take away the pain! Her journey to heaven had begun. God was definitely in the room with us. His presence was felt as we began to read the Bible and to pray. That had been Mother's only request.

I felt so fortunate that we hadn't missed out on the true value of life. We'd stopped in the midst of our hectic schedules and listened to one who was dying. What we heard was worth all that we had been through. Now, fortunately, much of what Mother represented belonged to us.

Sandy and I sat on either side of her bed holding her hands. We were given a precious opportunity, a privilege few people enjoy, as we sat by her side waiting for the transition from life, through death, into eternity. Soon God would call her home and say, " . . . Well done, thou good and faithful servant: thou hast been faithful over a few things, I will make thee ruler over many things: enter thou into the joy of thy lord" (Matthew 25:21). I could almost hear his voice and see him waiting for her. When she left, we would stay behind with treasured memories and hope for the time that we would meet again.

With no hesitation, I looked Mother directly in the eyes and said, "Mother, I think Jesus is calling you home today." I recognized a faint nod as her eyes caught mine. "I have to talk to you about something before you go." As sick as she was, she remained interested in what I had to say. "You and I both know that you are going to go to heaven and will spend all eternity there. I would like to have a memorial service for you. There will be many people there who don't have the confidence that we have. I would like your permission to tell them where you are and to tell them that you want to meet them there someday and then explain how that can happen."

Her response was positive.

I continued to read the Bible, especially the verses about heaven. Everyone in the room was still, caught up in his own private grief. Though absorbed in the words, I remained aware of what was happening around me. Mother's breathing was growing shallow and still. I couldn't bring myself to look at her expressionless eyes gazing straight ahead. Sandy asked me to read the Twenty-third

Psalm. At the close of the chapter, Mother drew her last breath. Her death was neither terrifying nor alarming. Rather, it was the picture of perfect acceptance.

As we encircled her bed with our love, our tears flowed unrestricted. I looked at Mother, closed her delicate blue eyes with my hands, kissed her cheek one final time, and said, "Good-bye, Mother, I love you." It was too late to thank her for the privilege that the past four years had been, but somehow I sensed she knew.

I stood for a moment watching everyone's sorrow, and my eyes met Ted's as he wept freely and unashamedly. Then Lee, Sandy's husband, came over and he and Ted embraced as they shared their loss together. Soon Ted reached for me and we left the room, leaving Sandy and her family to grieve alone.

We'd been given an invaluable legacy, an intense experience of love and tragedy as Mother had captured our hearts. God had allowed us to care for a fragile human being who had once been a child and grown into adulthood, who'd experienced being a wife, a mother, and a grandmother. She had known both poverty and riches. She had known what it was like to live and now she knew about life after death. Mother was a beautiful combination of many roles. She had caused us, because of her life and because of her affliction, to become better people.

Her life was not in vain.

> To everything there is a season, and a time to every purpose under the heaven:
>
> A time to be born, and a time to die; a time to plant, and a time to pluck up that which is planted;
>
> A time to kill, and a time to heal; a time to break down, and a time to build up;
>
> A time to weep, and a time to laugh; a time to mourn, and a time to dance;
>
> A time to cast away stones, and a time to gather stones together; a time to embrace, and a time to refrain from embracing;
>
> A time to get, and a time to lose; a time to keep, and a time to cast away;
>
> A time to rend, and a time to sew; a time to keep silence, and a time to speak;
>
> A time to love, and a time to hate; a time of war, and a time of peace (Ecclesiastes 3:1-8).

9

A Memorial Celebration

Verily, verily, I say unto you, He that heareth my word, and believeth on him that sent me, hath everlasting life, and shall not come into condemnation; but is passed from death unto life (John 5:24).

. . . and so shall we ever be with the Lord . . . comfort one another with these words (1 Thessalonians 4:17b, 18).

Four years had passed since we'd taken Mother from the nursing home to live with us for those predicted "three weeks," and even though all along we'd prepared ourselves for this moment, I felt suddenly stricken with an emptiness.

Four years is a long time. We'd spent many hours together and yet I'd never told Mother all that I wanted her to know. Now she was gone and it was too late to tell her how much I would miss her.

How could I have spoken those words as she lay on her deathbed waiting to be freed, finally unencumbered from the weight of illness that had been with her for so long? That would have been cruel and selfish.

Today she was free at last. Her name had been called and she was in heaven with her beloved Savior. I was left behind, wondering what it must be like.

Her room, once filled with loving activity, was now shrouded in stillness. For a moment I allowed myself to fall into grief, searching and questioning why I'd permitted certain things to happen, circling back to the occasions I'd regretted, wanting to reconcile the wrong.

Then I recalled one cold winter morning . . . it had been about six-thirty and I'd entered Mother's room, as usual, to see if she needed me. Her eyes were bright, waiting for my arrival. She smiled gently and her room was filled with a soft pink glow. Looking out her bedroom window, we viewed a magnificent sight.

During the night there had been an ice storm and the trees were coated with a thin layer of ice that glistened like diamonds with the reflection of the pink sky as dawn beckoned a new day.

We were both struck by the beauty, picturing an artist at work in heaven creating this scene just for us. We talked about it and decided that it must be one of the rare glimpses that God allows during our lifetime to demonstrate to us what heaven will be like.

I realized again, as I had realized that winter morning, that dying, for a Christian, shouldn't be a time of sadness. When we have such a wonderful place awaiting us, we should be filled with anticipation knowing that much preparation has gone into the planning of our arrival.

If not for the blessed hope of spending eternity in heaven and the time when I'd see Mother again, I know I would have been overwhelmed by grief. Instead, I found myself rejoicing.

Four years ago God had touched my life. He gave me a very difficult situation and guided me every step of the way. He taught me many valuable lessons.

God's presence in my life was not meant to be a secret. Rather, it was to become a message of hope to anyone who would listen . . . a message I promised Mother would be spoken at the memorial service. Now it was time to concentrate my efforts on that celebration.

Beginning to write my thoughts on paper, I was fascinated by the torrent of impressions that came to mind. Several hours later I began to put these ideas into action.

We chose Tuesday to have a private interment since Saturday seemed the most suitable time for the memorial service.

For the rest of the week, Toni, Pastor Trump, and Pastor Dyer (minister of the church we had been attending recently) helped me make the necessary arrangements for the service. We were delighted as we thought of the prospect of this commemoration touching many lives.

All at once there seemed to be a million things to do. After working through an outline for the memorial "celebration" program, we ran to the printer for the completion of the bulletin. The finished product was beautiful, with dark blue print on pale blue paper; 1 Corinthians 13:4-7 was written directly under Mother's name on the cover. Inside were the order of service, a favorite poem of Mother's, and various verses of Scripture which outlined the plan of salvation. The program was handed to each attendee. We thought of it as a gift, something to take home.

The telephone rang continuously, and always on the other end was someone who cared. Flowers arrived, fruit baskets, cakes, and cheeses. It felt good to be so loved. But the cards and letters were the most special.

At 8 on the morning of the service, the phone rang. When I answered it I heard my brother's familiar voice.

"Hi, Sis," he said. "Guess where I am?"

I couldn't imagine, but a flutter of excitement went through me as he continued.

"I'm at the Philadelphia Airport!" he said excitedly.

It wouldn't have been the same without him. Now the entire family would be here to memorialize Mother's life on earth and celebrate her victory over death.

All of Mother's favorite hymns were played on the organ as people arrived. We remained in the lobby, greeting them as they entered the church. This promised to be a happy occasion. Over two hundred people attended. Each touched our lives with his presence.

After everyone was seated the service began with a beautiful prayer by one of our church deacons. He asked God's blessing upon all that was said and done, praying that others would be united in heaven because of the service. Following the prayer, the congregation stood together and sang a hymn of praise.

During the week I had asked three of the "nurses" to share some thoughts as a tribute to Mother. Their beautiful comments will remain in my heart forever.

Lorraine was the first one to tell of her reflections over the past four years.

Perceiving Mother as a frightened, unhappy person when she first met her, she told how she witnessed Mother's "laughter of relief" at the moment she accepted Christ into her heart and life. Lorraine spoke about the changes that occurred as a result of Mother's commitment and concluded that, though at first she was very apprehensive, " . . . knowing Betty Nottingham was one of the greatest privileges in my life. I really praise the Lord. I received so much more than I could ever have given."

Then Phyllis stepped up to the microphone and told how she had depended on the Lord to guide her in caring for Mother's physical needs. She told about feeling the presence of the Lord in Mother's room and how, after Mother was born again, she ministered to Phyllis's spiritual needs.

Phyllis said that before she met Mother she felt confident and somewhat prideful, but ended by saying, "I really feel humbled at knowing her. In spite of her disease, she taught me patience and love. She showed a real dependence on the Lord and a complete willingness to do his will. I love her and I miss her already, but I really feel peace at knowing that she's with the Lord."

Then Anne Hartman began by saying " . . . I didn't know Betty before she came to the Lord, so taking care of her was always a pleasure. In some homes, having a member of the family who needed constant care would tear the family apart. But, not this home. To me, their love for the Lord was shown in their love for Betty. I could never lift Betty, so I would always have to ask John, or Lisa, or Brooke to help me. They never once objected." Anne said she expressed to Mother that she felt she was unable to do the job well because she couldn't lift her by herself. Mother always reassured her by telling her, "You make a wonderful nurse."

"Every day, before I would leave," Anne continued, "she would look up over her window. There was a sign that said 'I love you.' She would look at the sign and smile at me and I would go over and kiss her good-bye and say, 'I love you.'" Then Anne's voice began to crack. Catching herself, she finished, "All of us who took care of her loved her and will miss her."

I truly believe the sincere, loving words that each of the women spoke touched not only my heart, but every heart in the audience.

After the song "New Jerusalem" was sung by a soloist from our church, Pastor Dyer read some verses of Scripture. Then Ted went to the podium. He shared a meaningful poem that had hung on Mother's wall, as well as some personal family reflections.

Following Ted, Pastor Trump and then Pastor Dyer gave warm and inspiring memorial messages, sharing with everyone how he or she could come to know Christ personally and have that wonderful relationship with God that Mother had enjoyed.

The service ended happily as everyone joined in singing another hymn. I noticed expressions of a true spirit of love and joy on the faces of our family and friends as they came to thank us.

Mother would've been so pleased! I could almost have seen her smiling and looking up at her "I love you" sign.

Following the service a crowd of people arrived at our house for a beautifully prepared buffet. The meal had been arranged by two dear friends, Helen and Sherron, who, along with other friends, neighbors, and members of our church, provided everything we needed. What a wonderful gift it had been not to have to think about the details of food preparation during this busy week.

Perhaps the most permanent tribute to Mother was a poem written by the man who led her to Christ, Pastor Ted Trump. His ability to express his thoughts in the form of poetry and his acute insight into Mother as a person touched us all very deeply.

The message, one I eventually printed into a bookmark and sent to friends and loved ones, poignantly expressed the purpose of Mother's life. . . .

> *God planned it before time began*
> *Betty Nottingham he'd secure,*
> *With his precious Son he bought her soul*
> *And made her salvation sure.*

By faith Christ's blood made her spotless,
His goodness put to her account;
The Spirit of God became her seal,
Her joy, her peace, and her fount.

He planned the day of her new birth
And the day she entered glory;
It's God who wrote the very first page,
Then made complete the story.

The moment Christ became her own
The angels of heav'n did rejoice;
And her saddened countenance, trans-
   formed,
Became her triumphant voice.

Unable to convey in words
The brightness and depth of her spirit,
Her face and eyes unfolded her heart;
Somehow she made you hear it.

Few are called to a task like hers,
Confined to a room and a bed;
But God provided family and friends,
So with much love she was fed.

There it was she would grow in grace
By his Word and communion fair;
Her calling to be intercession,
Coming from a heart of care.

She prayed for others in their need
As she went to the mercy seat;

And pleaded with God for his good will,
Placing requests at his feet.

Her joy and love, her countenance,
Became a standard to behold;
She removed the rights for our complaints
Pointing to a better mold.

Her face directed us to Christ,
Her eyes to a sign that said love;
Her suffering to the blessed hope that,
When complete, we'll meet above.

Epilogue

Dear Bonnie,

When Carlee called to tell me about your mother, all I could think of was our Father who chose April 25 for his miracle for her. I thought of him as the greatest doctor of all who used your mother and your friend, Toni, as his instruments. Many of us have seen the glory that came out of this illness but we will never know how many more hundreds of lives have been touched by this situation through your testimony.

Nevertheless, Bonnie, the empty bedroom and spot in your heart for your mother are not to be minimized. And so, we weep with you and pray that that void will be quickly filled with the love of Jesus Christ and the knowledge that your mother will have a new body. We think of you and all your family and the women who helped care for her these last four years.

With deepest sympathy,
Betty Kay

Dear Bonnie,

All our hearts are bound together in many different ways. The deepest way our hearts are bound is in human love, wherein lies the pain of our grief. As we mature and reflect upon it, we find that in those experiences we can find our deepest, truest nature in contrast to the more superficial moments of our life, when we go blithely on our way.

I entered into a deep, true experience in life, Bonnie, when I first heard of your testimony of love for your mother one year ago. Again, I discovered the depths of that love when I met your mother and shared a few moments with her. The clouds of busy life did not obscure what I had heard, seen, and felt.

She is a beautiful person and in her death, as Christians, we can see that there is grandeur in life and death. Dear Bonnie, I hope you find great solace and comfort in your family and friends—sharing especially those three precious days that you mentioned to me on Sunday. Family and friends became the sounding board of a heartache string that is being plucked.

The crowning glory of grief is that we grow in spirit, which no one can escape. Christ not only gives us new faith in life and new faith in the tasks he would have us do, but he gives us even a deeper faith in him.

Love to you and your family,
Sally Fitzpatrick

Dear Mrs. Jamison,

Once in a while an example of love in action and the true performance of the wonderful work comes across the horizon. In this gray-colored world such examples stand out like a beacon light for the rest of us.

I am a better person for having been part of this desperate problem and for having seen you and your family in action.

God bless,
Perry S. MacNeal, M. D.

To the Jamison family,

I can remember when Brooke's grandmother and I first met. I was a bit hesitant after Brooke told me about her grandmother's problem. I didn't know what to say. At the time, she was living in Barton Run and not confined to a bed, but she had lost her speech. She was very nice and I could tell what she wanted to say just by looking into her eyes. One thing I'll never forget was a clear box filled with silver beads. When she showed it to me she turned it upside down and the beads went down levels of stairs. As we watched we would smile.

Later when Nanna moved in with the Jamisons I would see her quite frequently. Brooke and I would walk into her room at least once every time that I visited and we would talk for a while. Nanna always seemed very happy with

her life. She occasionally looked at the sign above
her window telling me that she loved me.

Another time Brooke and I visited Nanna,
she was reading her Bible. Brooke and I sat on
her bed and let her rest her eyes while we read
the Bible verses that she liked.

I think whenever I go to see Brooke that I will
miss her grandmother. She was a very wonderful
and special lady and I loved her. But, I know
it's good that she is with God now.

Susan Foster (age 15)

Dear Mrs. Jamison,

I just wanted to stop and say "thank you" for
all you taught me last weekend. I had never had
any contact whatsoever with the "death" of a
Christian and was blessed by the beauty of your
experience. Just your calm and gentle spirit was
a lesson in itself!

Mary Ellen

Dear Bonnie,

I just wanted to write and tell you my
thoughts about yesterday. It was a beautiful day
and my former fears of funerals were washed
away by the simplicity of this funeral.

It came to me this morning as I prayed, that
our family gathered together to rejoice at our sis-

ter's passing into eternal life with our Lord. It really did touch me and I shall always remember that. My fear is gone; I know I have been blessed.

I will keep you in my prayers that God will comfort you in the future days. I watched you yesterday with all that love in your eyes for your mother. I know there will be many times you will miss her presence. I have also been blessed with a loving, beautiful mother who is not only parent, but friend. I pray the Lord will give me the same strength I saw in you if I should ever need it.

> *Love you all,*
> *Aunt Ann and Uncle Bob*

Dear Bonnie,

When my mother went to be with the Lord a friend sent this item to me that she had received in the loss of her husband. It truly touched my heart. I thought it also would comfort your heart now. . . .

Just think of stepping on shore and finding it heaven!
Of touching a hand and finding it God's!
Of breathing new air and finding it celestial!
Of waking up in glory and finding it home!

> *Love in our Lord,*
> *Sue Atkinson*

Suggested Reading

The Four Spiritual Laws, Campus Crusade for Christ, Inc., 1965.

Handbook of Today's Religions: Understanding the Cults, Josh McDowell and Don Stewart, Here's Life Publishers, Inc., 1982.

Larson's Book of Cults, Bob Larson, Tyndale House Publishers, 1984.

The Mind Benders, Jack Sparks, Thomas Nelson, Publishers, Inc. 1977.

(For material on Christian Science contact Christian Way, Former Christian Scientists for Truth through Jesus Christ, P.O. Box 1675, Lancaster, CA 93539.)

Other Living Books Best-sellers

WHAT WIVES WISH THEIR HUSBANDS KNEW ABOUT WOMEN by James Dobson. The best-selling author of *DARE TO DISCIPLINE* and *THE STRONG-WILLED CHILD* brings us this vital book that speaks to the unique emotional needs and aspirations of today's woman. An immensely practical, interesting guide. 07-7896 $2.95.

HINDS' FEET ON HIGH PLACES by Hannah Hurnard. A classic allegory of a journey toward faith that has sold more than a million copies! 07-1429 $3.50.

MORE THAN A CARPENTER by Josh McDowell. A hard-hitting book for people who are skeptical about Jesus' deity, his resurrection, and his claims on their lives. 07-4552 $2.95.

LOOKING FOR LOVE IN ALL THE WRONG PLACES by Joe White. Using wisdom gained from many talks with young people, White steers teens in the right direction to find love and fulfillment in a personal relationship with God. 07-3825 $2.95.

ROCK by Bob Larson. A well-researched and penetrating look at today's rock music and rock performers, their lyrics, and their life-styles. 07-5686 $2.95.

GIVERS, TAKERS, AND OTHER KINDS OF LOVERS by Josh McDowell and Paul Lewis. This book bypasses vague generalities about love and sex and gets right to the basic questions: Whatever happened to sexual freedom? What's true love like? Do men respond differently than women? If you're looking for straight answers about God's plan for love and sexuality, this book was written for you. 07-1031 $2.50.

THE POSITIVE POWER OF JESUS CHRIST by Norman Vincent Peale. All his life the author has been leading men and women to Jesus Christ. In this book he tells of his boyhood encounters with Jesus and of his spiritual growth as he attended seminary and began his world-renowned ministry. 07-4914 $3.95.

MOUNTAINS OF SPICES by Hannah Hurnard. Here is an allegory comparing the nine spices mentioned in the Song of Solomon to the nine fruits of the Spirit. A story of the glory of surrender by the author of *HINDS' FEET ON HIGH PLACES*. 07-4611 $3.50.

NOW IS YOUR TIME TO WIN by Dave Dean. In this true-life story, Dean shares how he locked into seven principles that enabled him to bounce back from failure to success. Read about successful men and women—from sports and entertainment celebrities to the ordinary people next door—and discover how you too can bounce back from failure to success! 07-4727 $2.95.

HOW TO BE HAPPY THOUGH MARRIED by Tim LaHaye. One of America's most successful marriage counselors gives practical, proven advice for marital happiness. 07-1499 $2.95.

The books listed are available at your bookstore. If unavailable, send check with order to cover retail price plus $1.00 per book for postage and handling to:

Christian Book Service
Box 80
Wheaton, Illinois 60189

Prices and availability subject to change without notice. Allow 4–6 weeks for delivery.